EDUCATION FOR
MODERN MAN

A New Perspective

Education
F O R Modern Man
A New Perspective

SIDNEY HOOK

New Enlarged Edition

NEW YORK
HUMANITIES PRESS
1973

*Originally Published in 1963.
Reprinted 1973 by Humanities
Press, Inc. by Arrangement
with the Author*

NEW   ENLARGED   EDITION

Library of Congress Cataloging in Publication Data

Hook, Sidney, 1902–
    Education for modern man.

    Reprint of the ed. published by Knopf, New York,
in series: Borzoi books in education.
    1. Education––Aims and objectives. 2. Teaching.
I. Title.
[LB875.H72 1973]   370.1   73-9966
ISBN 0-391-00317-8

Printed in the United States of America

TO THE STUDENTS
I HAVE KNOWN

"*Education which is not modern shares the fate of all organic things that are kept too long.*"   ALFRED NORTH WHITEHEAD

"*The way out of scholastic systems that make the past an end in itself is to make acquaintance with the past a means of understanding the present.*"   JOHN DEWEY

CONTENTS

EDUCATION FOR MODERN MAN

A New Perspective

INTRODUCTION

RECESSIONS, revolutions, war and the necessity of preserving peace in a free world have placed the question of educational philosophy once more on the agenda of history. The accelerated pace of technological discovery, the challenge of communism, and the development of the American economy have raised the question to central importance. The immediate necessities of institutional planning to meet changing conditions have made it acute. In consequence, a great discussion has been raging throughout the land for almost two decades over the nature, content, and goals of education.

This stir and ferment has spread far beyond the narrow boundaries of professional circles in education. American philosophers, until now largely indifferent to educational issues, have been rediscovering the truth of John Dewey's claim that philosophy in the largest sense is "a general theory of education." Key government officials are drawing up blueprints for educational reconstruction. State aid to schools is developing thin theoretical threads that may in time control the distribution of support. Newspaper editors and columnists have launched campaigns to influence instruction. Some churches are beginning to eye the schools as long neglected territory into which to carry doctrines of salvation. The army and navy are evaluating our educational services in relation to what they conceive to be the military needs and tasks of tomorrow. Largescale industry is making plans in which the schools, on the vocational and the technological side, have a significant role. Even business—to use a term broad enough to cover the ubiquitous real-estate associations—has altered the character of its traditional interest in education. In the past, business viewed education primarily from the standpoint of its bearing on the tax rate. Now it is directly concerned not only with the costs of tax-supported and tax-exempt schools but with the *content* of schooling.

In short, education as never before is front-page news. This would perhaps be the healthiest and most encouraging sign in American education were it not marred by a tendency to exploit educational issues and proposals for purposes of sensationalism. Too often educational news is handled like a crime story. But even this is a small price to pay if it enables everybody to understand that education is everybody's business.

The starting-point for almost all participants in the modern debate is the deplorable condition of education on all levels above the kindergarten. As we rise higher in the educational scale, criticism becomes more vehement and focuses sharply on the colleges and universities. There is an impressive unanimity about the educational state of affairs in these pivotal institutions. Whatever a liberal education is, few American colleges offer it. Despite the well advertised curricular reforms in a few of our leading colleges, by and large the colleges of the country present a confused picture of decayed classical curriculums, miscellaneous social science offerings, and narrowing vocational programs—the whole unplanned and unchecked by leading ideas. What one finds in most colleges cannot be explained in terms of a consciously held philosophy of education, but rather through the process of historical accretion. The curriculum of a typical college is like a series of wandering and intersecting corridors opening on rooms of the most divergent character. Even the cellar and attic are not where one expects to find them.

This process of historical accretion has many causes but few good reasons. It is the result of divergent pressures. The inertia of tradition and the irrepressible wish to keep abreast of the times; the impact of an economy in which everything, including education, must pay for itself and the desire to prepare for anticipated leisure; the demands of legislatures, special interest groups, genuine patriots, patrioteers and the requirements set by the professional guilds—are some of the pressures which have dictated the patterns of higher education. And not least among them are vested departmental interests. Some subjects continue to be taught because those who teach them can teach nothing else.

It is easy, therefore, to draw up a depressing and true indictment of the current educational scene. But it would be a sad mistake to judge an educational philosophy or school of thought by its criticisms of the status quo. The error would be analogous to that committed by those who judged totalitarianism only in the light of the impressive criticisms its spokesmen uttered of the weaknesses of parliamentary democracy and the evils of capitalism—criticisms that were largely drawn from the writings of principled democrats and socialists. Criticism is, of course, important, for where nothing needs to be criticized nothing need be done. But the proposed cures or reforms are much more important, for they may turn out to be worse than the disease.

Criticism of the current evils of education often suffers from two oversights. Where the present is unfavorably compared with the past, the details of achievement and failure of the present are well known but those of the past are not. Consequently, the most exaggerated virtues may be attributed to past education with no more evidence than the inner conviction that it must have been so. Or a cluster of eminent figures of the past is selected as proof of the quality of the education of their time. By the same logic, one can argue from the life of Lincoln and others that no formal education is the best education. But the greatest error is to discount the fact—even when it is noted

—that modern education faces a task that no previous system of education confronted, viz., the schooling of the entire population. Where education even on the highest levels is no longer a leisure-class privilege but a universal right, comparisons can establish little of significance. Good criticism, even when it embraces the educational ideals of the past, must be guided by the specific possibilities, always limited, of the present.

In the following discussion, we shall not only make constructive proposals for the improvement of American education, but shall consider the character of some of the major challenges currently being hurled against American educational practices.

The discussion will revolve around four generic questions:

(1) What should the aims or ends of education be, and how should we determine them?

(2) What should its skills and content be, and how can they be justified?

(3) By what methods and materials can the proper educational skills and content be most effectively communicated in order to achieve the desirable ends?

(4) How are the ends and means of education related to a democratic social order?

A satisfactory answer to these questions should provide a satisfactory answer to the problem of what constitutes a liberal education in modern times.

I am indebted to Professor Richard Courant, Bertrand Russell, and Albert Einstein for permission to quote the letters printed in the text.

The proposed curriculum of studies in Chapter Six and the program in Chapter Eight are based upon an experiment conducted some years ago in the Unified Studies Division of the Washington Square College of Liberal Arts and Science, New York University.

To John Dewey, Horace M. Kallen, Gail Kennedy, Ernest Nagel, and Ann Hook I owe the stimulus of many conversations about modern education. Specific acknowledgments will be found in the text.

SIDNEY HOOK

South Wardsboro, Vermont
August, 1945
November, 1962

Chapter 1

THE CONTEMPORARY SCENE IN EDUCATION: CHALLENGE AND OPPORTUNITY

EVEN MORE than when this book was originally published, American education today is marked by confusion, uncertainty, and heated debate. A touch of hysteria has infected the discussion of what, in the memory of many adults, was customarily regarded as a boring subject. The most preposterous claims are being made for new programs of educational reform—a reform mainly directed toward undoing the work of an earlier generation of reformers. The adjectives "basic," "essential," "realistic," recur in an extensive literature that warrants the designation of "educational fundamentalism" as much for its tone of extremism and unction as for its promise of national salvation.

Leading political figures of actual and potential Presidential rank, as well as humble county and municipal officials, sensing an awakened public interest in education, have tossed off judgments about the deplorable state of American education and offered remedies to restore it to its presumably once-healthy condition when they were at school.

The post-war surge of interest in education reached its crescendo when the Soviet Union sent its first Sputnik into space—and American public opinion into a tail spin of fear and self-doubt. It would hardly be an exaggeration to say that Before Sputnik and After Sputnik mark two ages in popular American thinking about education. The nation came out of the shock to its pride and self-confidence produced by the glittering orbit of the Soviet satellites with a frenzied scramble for educational short cuts which would restore its much vaunted technological superiority. This reaction was not merely an expression of vanity or chauvinist feeling. For with good reason there was widespread apprehension lest the Soviet scientific triumphs betoken a growing nuclear missile capacity which, in the service of a declared hostile ideology, would threaten the very survival of the United States and therewith of the free world. Crash programs were called for to produce more engineers and scientists, to teach intensive courses in mathematics and sciences at all educational levels, to prune the curriculum of high schools and colleges of the dry rot of needless cultural courses, and to favor the gifted students by accelerating their educational development.

The concern was commendable, the panic was not. Some desirable programs have been developed. These programs, however, do not follow from the large claims that have been made about the necessity of a return to "basic" education and from the wholesale condemnation of existing educational practices but rather from an increasing awareness of the impact of mounting technological change upon contemporary culture and the urgency of the problems such change creates—problems which cannot be solved by more knowledge of the natural sciences but only by a wisdom nurtured in critical studies of the social, political, and humanistic disciplines. Most societies in periods of crisis tend to look for scapegoats and, by and large during the last decade, the professional educator has been the sacrificial object of crusading zealots for the one right educational approach. In order to differentiate him from teachers in other institutions of higher learning, who have happily awakened to the realization that they, too, are educators, despite the fact that precious few of them have ever thought hard or consistently about education, the professional educator has been dubbed an "educationist." This ugly word has acquired a certain disparaging connotation. An "educationist" is one who without knowing very much about any particular subject matter teaches the teachers of our children how to teach without overmuch concern whether our children really learn anything of consequence. The professional educators have been denounced as "self-serving paragons of mediocrity," who have imposed patterns of accreditation on the various local educational systems, making it impossible for teachers of the young to exercise their craft unless they enroll in certain prescribed courses in pedagogy. These courses are often characterized as irrelevant if not detrimental to a genuine teaching process whose fruits should be the acquisition of the skills of communication, familiarity with the cultural heritage of our civilization, and basic knowledge of the major intellectual disciplines.

I have no desire to defend the practices of our Schools of Education if only because of the feeble intellectual response, suggestive of deep lack of assurance in their life calling, their faculties have made to the concerted and persistent attacks upon them by their detractors. It goes without saying that any curriculum of educational studies can be improved. However, it makes much less sense to criticize Schools or Departments of Education for failing to teach the subject matter of the conventional disciplines, which is not their primary province, than to criticize liberal arts colleges or departments, which should have the chief responsibility for instruction in such courses, for failing to teach subject-matter courses properly. It is notorious that ability to teach, or even knowledge of the barest rudiments of good teaching, is not regarded as a prerequisite for teaching in the overwhelming majority of liberal arts institutions of the country.

Criticisms of modern American education, and of its agencies of professional education, have come from various sources—the academy, the Church and the churches, business, and the military. Different aspects of the current educational enterprise have aroused the ire of special groups but all have united in a full-throated polemic against the thinker held responsible for the major evils of American education—John Dewey.

On the one hundredth anniversary of his birth and only seven years after his death, the educational philosophy of John Dewey was condemned by the highest political authority in the United States. In a letter published in *Life* (March 15, 1959), President Eisenhower, who also served briefly as President of Columbia University, where John Dewey taught for more than a quarter-century, wrote: "Educators, parents and students must be continuously stirred up by the defects in our educational system. They must be induced to abandon the educational path that, rather blindly, they have been following as a result of John Dewey's teachings."

This criticism climaxed the offensive from opposite quarters of the ideological compass against Dewey's educational philosophy. Book upon book, article upon article still develops the same theme. Criticism of the multiple inadequacies of American education is coupled with large, vague, but forthright attacks on John Dewey as the prime cause of American failure. Even the Navy and Marines have been called in! One of the most strident books in this vein is Vice-Admiral Hyman Rickover's *Education and Freedom,* which should properly be entitled "Education for Victory in the Next War." It is both striking and significant that most of the criticism does not even attempt to come to grips with Dewey's central educational doctrines. Instead it merely deplores the faults and weaknesses of American education, in the light of the threat to freedom's future implicit in Soviet technological advance and our relative failure to meet this threat with assurance and adequacy.

For all their legitimate, if newly awakened, concern with education today, one gets the impression that most vocal latter-day critics do not themselves exhibit that value of *conscien-*

tiousness in their criticism which they would have our schools stress in their curriculum. They seem to be looking for excuses for our predicament rather than searching for its genuine causes. If they had actually read Dewey instead of denouncing him, they would have observed that he himself was a lifelong critic of American education, and that on occasion his criticism extended even to that small private sector of American education which was "progressive" in orientation and had originally taken its point of departure from his principles. More important still, it was John Dewey who long ago foresaw and warned against the very elements which have produced the crisis of our times and set off the current hysteria about the state of American education.

It is generally agreed that the main outlines of our crisis were shaped by the convergence of two great phenomena. The first is the transformative effects of science and technology on society, industry, and culture. The second is the emergence of Communist totalitarianism as an expanding imperialism which sees in the United States the chief foe to its crusade for world domination.

During the last fifty years of his life, Dewey defined our age as the age of the scientific revolution. He called upon educators to take note of the vast implications of the scientific revolution and of the changes it produced in our way of life. He urged a searching inquiry into the institutions, principles, and methods necessary to channel and master these changes in the interest of inclusive and humane ends. Calling for improvement of science instruction in elementary schools more than a half-century ago, he wrote: "I believe the attitude toward the study of science is, and should be, fixed during the earlier years." He took scientific knowledge as his paradigm of knowledge; and he proposed that its basic *logic* or *pattern* of thinking, as distinct from specific techniques and methods, be adopted as a norm in thinking wisely about political and social affairs. Some of the critics who have joined the outcry that Dewey has ill prepared American schools for the challenge of our scientific and technological world are the very ones who not long ago charged him with "scientism," with placing undue emphasis upon the mode of scientific experience while slighting other modes. The simple truth is that no one who took Dewey's educational ideas seriously would have been surprised by recent technological advances.

The same is true for the other major explosive element in the current situation. During the last twenty years of his life, and most especially during World War II when the Soviet Union was being hailed by professional humanists and scientists, as well as by leading admirals and generals and politicians, as a trusted ally of the democratic powers, Dewey described the nature of the Communist threat to the free world. He did not wait for the Kremlin to put a satellite in the sky to recognize the portents of disaster. He proclaimed them when the Kremlin established its satellites on earth—and even before then. He called for an intelligent foreign policy based on realistic understanding of the nature of Communism, which he had studied intensively from the time of the infamous Moscow Trials in the mid-thirties. The time to prepare for the peace, he wrote, is when Stalin needs us, not when Stalin has triumphed.

It is the absence of this intelligent foreign policy, for which the politicians, generals, and admirals are chiefly responsible, that accounts for the particular crisis that today agitates Admiral Rickover and his confreres. During the last war, the American educational system was no better, and in some respects much worse, than it is today. But we had enough political gumption to realize what the nature of Hitlerism was— and what its victory would mean to the prospects of freedom. We were able to introduce the emergency research programs which insured our victory.

This point is of crucial importance with respect to those who see in the scientific and technological character of Soviet education the cause of its engineering triumphs, the source of its ever growing strength and consequent danger to the free world, and a possible model for our own educational reorientation. The German educational system before World War II was much closer in structure, spirit, and technological emphasis to the current educational system of the USSR than to that of the U.S.A. Yet we were able to achieve feats of engineering and technical innovation which dwarfed the best efforts of the German scientific economy, whose achievements with respect to weapons research were not inconsiderable. The V-2 rocket was the basis of subsequent Soviet developments. Nonetheless, the German scientific community was unable to liberate atomic energy and fashion the bomb which would have put victory into Hitler's maniacal grasp. Despite efforts to make a virtue out of their failure, and to pass it off as a humanitarian act of renunciation, it was not for lack of trying that the German scientists made little progress in their quest. Every indictment currently made against the educational system of the United States could have been made with greater force and warrant against the educational system which prevailed in the United States during the thirties. And yet the greatest triumphs fell to us. No nation enjoyed more power to determine the course of world history than was possessed by the United States at the close of the war. Far from being an Achilles' heel, the educational system with all its inadequacies still possessed sufficient strength to permit the necessary improvisations.

What happened subsequently? Those responsible for political and defense policy failed to understand the nature of Communism and failed, therefore, to provide the leadership and vision required to contain the newer and more dangerous threat to freedom. They stumbled from error to error, from one improvisation to another, from appeasement to bluster. They were unable to take the initiative with intelligent policies because they lacked a clear grasp of nationalism, of Communism, and of the impact of the new scientific revolution upon the world.

I should not like to be misunderstood as implying that failures and successes in foreign policy flow *directly* from educational philosophy or practice. But precisely such a proposition seems to be implied by the grand panjandrums of the anti-Dewey parade who are convulsed with fury at what they call progressive education. For what they really are deploring is our truly serious condition vis-à-vis the growing power of the totalitarian world—a serious condition that testifies to the defect of political intelligence, and sometimes of elementary political knowledge, on the part of those responsible for that policy in the past. If education is relevant to this question, we must look to the education of those in strategic places and command posts. Have those who have neglected the needs of scientific military defense from Pearl Harbor to the present, who have systematically neglected the opportunities for democratic ideological warfare, who have failed to make the United States the leader of the world movement for colonial liberation—have all those politicians, generals, and admirals been brought up on progressive education, or in the spirit of Dewey's educational philosophy?

Admiral Rickover and some other critics of Dewey seem to be interested in an education which primarily will help us win the next war. If Dewey's educational philosophy had truly guided American education and inspired the architects of American foreign policy, they would have understood the nature and dangers of communism. Their programs during and after the war would have been geared to the double-faced problem of how to avoid a world war and yet preserve and extend the heritage of a free society. For this is a corollary of the basic educational aim of Dewey's philosophy: education for creative intelligence in a world of peace and freedom and danger—yes, *danger*.

Despite those who tax him with lapsing into a cheerful and

complacent naturalism because man is "in" and "of" nature, the world as viewed from Dewey's philosophical perspective has at least two generic traits of outstanding importance for the condition of man. He marked them conspicuously on the "metaphysical" map of life he projected for human guidance. They are danger and openness, or precariousness and opportunity. Whoever turns to the pages of *Experience and Nature* will observe the emphasis upon the precarious; whoever ponders the upshot of any of Dewey's philosophical works will find that they alert us to the presence of possibilities arising from indefeasible change. The world we live in is a world of danger which fluctuates in intensity but is always present. It is also a world of opportunity, sometimes narrow and restricted to grim alternatives; sometimes broad and multiple in its possibilities of choice. As a rule, the dangers are more obvious to us than the opportunities because the latter are a function of our intelligence. They have to be sought for, made, or discovered. In a precarious world, thinking diminishes danger by enlarging opportunity. An education which equips man to live a significant life in a dangerous world cannot be the "soft education" which Rickover and the others properly disdain. Nor must it necessarily be only the "hard education" of technical, mathematical, and scientific courses which they currently are crying up. The world may be dangerous not only because of our ignorance of advanced mathematics and physics, but because of our ignorance of elementary politics, economics, and social psychology. Without genuine *political* understanding, the leaders of the Western world could not prevent Communism's post-war expansion, even if they possessed the mathematical and scientific knowledge of an Einstein—whose own political judgments, alas, were extremely naive and often tragically mistaken.

There is no gainsaying the shortcomings of what is known as "progressive education." They were trenchantly criticized by Dewey himself in his *Education and Experience* in the early thirties, long before the reaction against it set in, and they have been considered in the body of the present work. I myself once threw a meeting of progressive educators into disorder by suggesting that among the basic resources of the educational process are "books." But no movement should be judged by its periphery of faddists. The basic assumptions of progressive education concerning the nature of educational experience and learning, and the meaning and implication of democracy in education, remain intact in the light of the enlarged knowledge we have won about man, nature, and historical experience. They have not been undermined by criticism. Nor is it even true that the American school system by and large reflected progressive principles in any fundamental way, either in Dewey's time or in our own. Here and there some of its teachings were applied to the physical organization of the school. The discipline of the classroom was relaxed so that students were no longer required to behave like little automata, which was sometimes mistakenly interpreted to mean a degree of permissiveness that would be hard to justify even toward the emotionally disturbed. Massive doses of the *terminology* of progressive education were injected into the ways educators talked about the processes of teaching and learning but the enormous bulge in population, by swelling the size of normal classes in most metropolitan centers, made it impossible to pay realistic attention to the individual needs of precisely those students who could have profited most from an intelligent progressive approach.

I shall disregard the chorus of educational slogans which have burst upon us in recent years and consider some of the chief schools of thought which have advanced the claim that they possess the key to desirable educational reforms. One of the most articulate of these schools is neo-Thomism. To the extent that it makes claims to provide orientation for secular

education, much of what it professes has already been advanced
in the writings of Robert M. Hutchins, Mortimer Adler and
the architects of the St. John's College curriculum. The argument of the original edition of this book seems to me to be
sufficient to indicate the radical inadequacy of this philosophy
of education for our times. Its fundamental fallacy may be
illustrated by an analysis of some key metaphors employed
by Dr. Adler in defense of his position that all students, despite
their differences in capacity, should be required to complete
the same curriculum of liberal arts studies. In his *Liberal Education in an Industrial Democracy*, he writes:

Human differences in capacity for education can be thought of in
terms of containers of different sizes. Obviously a half-pint jar
cannot hold as much liquid as a quart or gallon jar. Now the poorly
endowed child is like the half-pint jar, and the gifted child like the
quart or gallon container.[1]

He concludes not only that each container must be filled up
to the brim but that each must be filled with the same rich,
thick "cream of liberal education."

The comparison of children to different measures, reinforced
by the conception of teaching as the *pouring* of the same stuff
into passive containers, expresses a point of view hard to recon-
cile with what we know about children as organic creatures
and learners whose differential responses determine not merely
what they can absorb but what they can assimilate. Metaphors
are innocent when they betray only our bias. They are dangerous when they distort the subject matter of inquiry. The
task of educational inquiry is to find and offer the appropriate
curricular nourishment for different types of organisms that
will enable them to achieve the full measure of their growth

[1] Mortimer Adler: *Liberal Education in an Industrial Democracy* (San
Francisco: Industrial Indemnity Co.; 1957), p. 35.

and health. That curricular nourishment may be the same or it may be varied. The test of its adequacy is the *function* it performs in the life and development of the student. Different curricular fare may perform the same function in awakening the powers of the student and arousing his intellectual interests. But what performs the same function need not necessarily give the same results. A dull child will never be able to read as well or as intelligently as a bright child, and an ordinary child will never be able to play as well as a musically gifted child. But both children can be so educated that each enjoys reading and music to some degree. Both can acquire something of the grace and taste associated with the liberal arts. They may not be able to do so by studying the same subjects, even though the study of some subjects will be common to them.

Simple justice to Dr. Adler requires that I quote a further passage in which he explicates the metaphor of the different containers in a way that departs from the whole emphasis of his previous writings in education which justified an identical curriculum for all students.

The main point of my illustration is missed if you make the mistake of identifying the cream of liberal education with the traditional books, subjects, or tasks which once were the substance of liberal schooling when it was given only to the few, and which still constitute, in my judgment, the best materials to use in the case of the more gifted children. *The best education for the best becomes the best education for all, not by means of the same materials and methods, but rather by achieving the same effect with all children through using whatever materials and methods produce the same results at different levels of capacity.*[2]

This passage, particularly the sentence I have italicized, departs so radically from the letter and spirit of the traditional philosophy of education that it may legitimately be interpreted as

[2] Ibid., p. 38.

one of the most dramatic, even if unannounced, conversions to the philosophy of progressive education.

A second tendency in contemporary American educational thought emphasizes the intellectual toughness of its approach to the problems of teaching and learning. Its stress falls on the "hard" subjects—the sciences and mathematics—and whatever else is required to keep students alert to developments in these fields. It expects this knowledge to become the basis for ready acquisition of professional skills which will enable the average product of our schools to perform the specialized tasks which industry, technology, and war may demand if the nation is to survive.

It is one thing to demand a crash program to meet an emergency. It is quite another to erect a philosophy of education upon considerations relevant only to an emergency, and to impose a pattern perhaps suitable for a country first entering into the age of industrialization upon the generality of students. But what if the emergency is "permanent" or long drawn out? In that case both the pressures of national need and the rewards for specialized talent will tend to create the necessary corps of specialists. Any intelligent system of education must allow for improvisations: no one, however, can be so sure of the future as to plan for all of them now. What may be required may be so different from what the envisagement of a permanent emergency calls for today that the specialists may find themselves educated into a state of trained incapacity.

As the body of the text of this book will show, modern education is unworthy of its name if it does not expose all students to scientific education. But such scientific education, before the period of specialization has begun, must be conceived as integral to liberal education and not a mere propaedeutic to technological training. This is particularly true for education in a free society which does not merely aim to produce the craftsmen and the fashioners of the means to achieve ends laid down by the ruling political group but strives to develop citizens critically aware of these ends and capable and willing to evaluate them. Technicians and specialists, whether in pure or applied disciplines, are not notorious for their sensitiveness to the political and cultural values of the society which gives them a highly favored status. In the Soviet Union, which is rapidly becoming the educational model even of many who abominate the Soviet social system, the voices of liberation, to the extent that they have been heard, have been the voices of the poets, dramatists, and humanists. When a literary or humanist mind speaks up for creative freedom against bureaucratic suppression, he speaks for all who seek new visions of truth in any field; when scientists, as they often do in totalitarian countries, demand freedom of inquiry untrammeled by party dogma, they sometimes tend to narrow their claims to their own or kindred fields, and usually accompany their demands with assurances that scientific freedom will yield better practical results. They are more often prepared to accede to suppression of truths told out of season in politics and culture than are defenders of creative freedom in art and literature.

History has shown, alas, that freedoms are *not* indivisible—but the strategic freedoms which hold the greatest promise for the greatest cultural freedom, in the most comprehensive sense of the term culture, are the political, social, and ethical freedoms that address themselves critically to the values and institutions of a society. It is these freedoms which totalitarian societies are the last to grant despite all their thaws. The rulers of such societies may in the future recognize freedom of inquiry in the natural sciences in order to survive or to conquer. They may even tolerate a kind of *Narrenfreiheit*—the freedom of a favored few to satirize their foibles with the license of court jesters. But they cannot permit criticism which calls their wisdom into question, which exposes the vital root

of personal and bureaucratic vested interest in the pious plati-
tudes about the common good or public policy that mask
oppression.

These considerations point up the inadequacy of Sir Charles
Snow's assumption that there are two cultures—scientific and
humanistic—whose cleavage threatens the existence of Western
society. This simple division of cultures may be challenged
on various grounds. From the point of view of the spirit of
inquiry and the search for new realms of meaning and truth
there is a profounder difference between the technological
and engineering sciences, on the one hand, and the theoretical
sciences, on the other, than between the latter and humanistic
studies. From the point of view of subject matters, there is the
entire range of political and social studies, including history,
disregard of which leads to irresponsibility among humanists
and brutality among scientists as soon as they draw consequences from their large and bright ideas for everyday practice. The humanist who is devoid of political sophistication,
who opposes the extension of science and scientific methods
to the problems of underdeveloped or industrially backward
countries on the ground that it tears the seamless fabric of
tribal customs and values and destroys the intimate circle of
communication "among the women around the village well,"
is a sentimentalist. The scientist who knows that machines can
be humanly liberating if properly controlled but fails to realize
that democratic consensus and participation are the primary
demands of free men may well end up by becoming the scientific advisor or henchman of the bureaucrat or dictator who
claims to know what is best for his charges better than they
do themselves.

Our schools must do many things but they will not teach
us to understand other men and cultures, other idea patterns
and ideologies, merely by adding courses in mathematics and
physics to the curriculum. Let us recall that traditional humanists and scientists were helpless in grasping the phenomena

of Fascism and Communism. Natural scientists cannot predict the social consequences of the impact of science on different cultures. With some notable exceptions, they have been tragically inept in anticipating the responses of the Kremlin to reasonable proposals for the international control of nuclear weapons, from the time when the United States, as a consequence of the urging of leading scientists, offered to abandon its monopoly of atomic power to a world authority. The processes of social change have been just as opaque to humanists of predominantly literary culture as to natural scientists even to those humanists literate enough about thermodynamics and atomic physics to merit Snow's approval. Dr. Leavis, Snow's vitriolic critic, apparently believes that the gospel according to D. H. Lawrence is guidance enough to solve the multiple social and political problems of our world. The sneers that natural scientists sometimes direct against the so-called social sciences reveal a too narrow conception of science and an underestimation of the amount of knowledge, vague and inexact as it may be, which we already bring to bear in controlling and understanding human behavior. The issues of war and peace, freedom and enslavement, international law and government in a world of cultural and social diversity are issues central to what may legitimately be called the "third" culture. No reform of education that banishes intensive study of these and allied themes to the periphery of the curriculum is acceptable, particularly in a democratic society which may find itself at bay before the onslaught of totalitarianism.

From a more restricted pedagogical point of view a curriculum of "hard subjects" has a narrowing effect on the educational experience and growth of students. The very use of terms like "hard" and "soft" is misleading. They do not designate intrinsic properties of any subject matter. Subjects are hard or soft with respect to *how* they are taught and *to whom*. The present use of the terms seems to reflect an assessment of current interests among students brought up by a generation of teachers who made no notable effort to present mathematics and science in an exciting or dramatic way. The "easy" subjects—humanities and the social studies—possessed very few reliable yardsticks to measure intellectual growth and competence in their fields.

The great difficulty of a "crash program" which seeks to glamorize the subjects of mathematics and science as strategic to national survival is that it does not guarantee that students will be left with a permanent intellectual interest in these disciplines on which they can capitalize professionally later. Its effect is much more likely to arouse a profound distaste for, if not aversion to, these subjects among gifted students who are slow starters with respect to them or whose natural gifts lie in other directions although they possess sufficient intelligence to master the scientific elements. Were the sciences and mathematics taught with greater skill in the normal course of instruction, a far greater number of students could be permanently attracted to these studies than would be processed by the emerging programs set up in great haste and sometimes taught by those who are indifferent to the needs of the students.

The danger of any type of education which stresses, before the normal age of differentiation and election, the centrality of the scientific and mathematical studies is its tendency to make for a narrow kind of instrumentalism which John Dewey would have been the first to repudiate. Such an education neglects the consummatory aspects of experience and the variety of skills and knowledge which enter into the acquisition of cultivated taste and judgment. Education oriented toward the "hard" subjects is almost always a preface to *professional* orientation and may turn out students who are educational barbarians—extremely competent in scientific research but extremely naive in political and social affairs. It is worth pondering the fact that the engineering students in Germany during the Weimar Republic whose curriculum consisted mainly of studies in science and mathematics were among the fiercest partisans of the Nazi movement, whereas those who worked in the pure sciences were more resistent to totalitarianism. The scarcity of opportunities for employment accounts in part for this phenomenon, but it does not explain the intensity of the differential response. It is safe to predict that if current emphasis on mathematical and scientific proficiency is intensified, and students who have less aptitude for these disciplines than for others are made to feel that they are not properly preparing for the Space Age of the Future, many will drop out and be lost to the educational process. Discouragement, resentment, self-depreciation are not the best incentives to educational effort.

That technical scientific education today gives students who are successfully subjected to it a vocational edge over others is not to be denied. The rewards for those who complete such training are higher than for those who undertake careers in the humanities or the social studies. But again, except in emergency situations, this kind of vocationalism, even at a superior level of skill and knowledge, is just as hostile to a program of liberal education as the more conventional varieties of vocationalism.

If present economic and social tendencies continue there is a risk that even vocational possibilities will be progressively reduced as automation is extended to the production of goods and services. The character of technological vocations will become more highly specialized as the number of vocations diminishes. Some economists even predict that in the foreseeable future, barring war, meaningful work in industry will become a luxury to be distributed to those who wish to escape the tedium and monotony of uncreative idleness, as a reward without any further monetary inducements. This presupposes a society in which automation provides adequate goods and services for all by means of machines which will design and produce other machines with hardly any investment of human labor. One need not take this fanciful picture altogether literally to recognize that it points a true and grim moral.

It goes without saying that any kind of education which warrants the adjective "liberal" must, indeed, give an important place to the subject matters of mathematics and science. But on the level of general education they cannot be permitted to dominate the curriculum with the claim that the chief end of education should be the education of the intellect or mind. Nor can we reject this onesidedness simply on the ground that it is the education of the whole person which should be the lodestar of educational effort. In the sloganized form in which it is often proclaimed, this antithesis between "the intellect" and "the whole man" is more misleading than fruitful even when we recognize that the contending positions express important insights. Can we educate for "intellect" or "mind" in a desirable way without educating for much else? Can we educate "the whole man" without educating a certain kind of man whose integral wholeness will differ from that of his neighbor?

The intellect or mind is not an abstract, disembodied power. It influences and is influenced by our emotions. It guides perception and is checked by perception. On the other hand, although all aspects of body and mind in a person are somehow related in a pattern of personality behavior, they do not all seem equally important in determining the characteristic Gestalt. They cannot all be developed and certainly not at the same time. Except when we encounter a Leonardo, we cannot avoid selecting and developing some powers at the cost of inhibiting the development of others. The concert pianist is not likely to be in a position to cultivate his skill as a pugilist for other reasons than his fear of damage to his hands. There simply is not enough time to develop all of our intellectual interests, not to speak of all our practical aptitudes. Development opens up new possibilities, but it is also true that it takes place through successive limitations of possibilities. If the development of the powers of cooking, fishing, and roller-skating get in the way of the development of the powers of reading, writing, and problem-solving, then the first must yield. So much for the development of the whole man!

Let us look at the mind in action. It is never found disembodied, but always immersed in concrete problems of finding out and exploring meanings. For example, what does it mean, educationally speaking, to develop the student's powers of thinking in the biological sciences? Anyone who sets out to teach his students to think in these fields is teaching them at the same time how to see, how to observe, how to use instruments, how to discipline impatience, how to curb the impulse to take short cuts. Is all this part of the mind? Trained observation in every field is an art. It is not merely *looking*, because it is guided by general ideas that structure the field of perception differently from what it appears to the open and innocent mind. Thinking about machines involves knowing how to make or use things. Thinking is not *merely* reasoning. Otherwise we would have to regard every paranoiac as a thoughtful man. It is not accidental that *thoughtful* and *sensible* are closely related. Chesterton once remarked that pure logic was the only thing an insane man had left.

What does it mean to think about a play, or about a poem, or about people? It means also to feel, to imagine, to conjure up a vision. Not *only* that but *also* that. Why is it that we often say to some thoughtless person, "Put yourself in his place"? To another, "You haven't got the feel or the hang of it"? To a third, "You understand everything about the situation except what really matters"? We do not convey truths by this way of speaking, but we help others to find the truth. If artists and musicians think, as well as music and art critics, their sensory discriminations must be relevant to the thinking they do. After all, we do speak of educated tastes. It is absurd, therefore, to say that the exclusive preoccupation of education should be the development or training of the mind.

Nonetheless, although the antithesis between these two points of view must be rejected, the accent has to fall on one rather than the other. To avoid the implicit-faculty psychology associated with the use of the term "mind," I prefer the term "intelligence." Intelligence suggests more than mere ratiocination. It suggests the ability to look for evidence, the competence to discern the likely places where it can be found, and the capacity to weigh it judiciously. The intelligent man knows when it is time to stop reasoning and to act, when it is time to stop experimenting and to declare his results. Of him one never says that he is educated beyond his capacities. He is wise rather than learned because he knows the uses and limits of learning.

For many years the phrases "democracy in education" and "education for democracy" have been shibboleths bandied about by writers more interested in declaring their allegiance than in clarifying ideas. Today these phrases are at a discount. As the swing toward the revival of traditional positions acquires momentum, many critics contend that the meaning given to these phrases in the writings of Dewey, and still more in the practices of progressive education which received his blessing, encourages, even if it does not explicitly approve, the habits of adjustment and conformity to existing mores, the cult of mediocrity, the fetish of equality, and the systematic denigration of intellectual excellence.

If these critics exhibited in their own thinking the intellectual sophistication whose alleged absence they deplore among "educationists," they could hardly be serious in their charge that the theory of experience which underlies the whole of Dewey's philosophy necessarily involves the adjustment of the individual to his society and his conditioning to its dominant ways and values. For this theory of experience which is rooted in modern biology and psychology, stresses the fact that human experience is a process of undergoing-and-selective reaction, that situations are not so much *given* as *taken*, that the self redetermines its environment as much as it is determined by it in a continuous process of interaction—or in a transactional history—which makes it possible for intelligent behavior to reform, redo, remake, and if necessary, revolutionize human society and man's life within it. An education which stresses conditioning students in their responses, or their adjustment to what appears like the status quo, can only succeed by inhibiting the creative moment, the potentially redirective phase of normal behavior. When critics like Admiral Rickover write: "The American people have never authorized the schools to replace education with life-adjustment training and behavioral conditioning; yet we have permitted the schools to experiment with Dewey's ideas for a long time," they convict themselves of gross unfamiliarity with the subject of their animadversions.

It would be a more legitimate, even if mistaken, criticism of Dewey to say that his stress on the development of intelligence is likely to lead to estrangement from society or opposition to it, to a desire to reform and transform it rather than to a willingness to accept it as it is. In order to be intelligent one must have ideas. To have ideas is to entertain alternatives, possibilities, visions of what may be. To have ideas one believes in is to be committed or ready to act on them. To act on them means introducing a directed change either in the environment or in ourselves. According to Dewey, we make our environment in part, because our response to it is a selective response depending upon our attention and interest. We make our environment *only in part* because we must accept most of it without thinking—thinking is done only on occasion—and because the results of all sane thinking must acknowledge the existence of what exercises compulsion upon what we do. But the world we live in, whether personal or public, private or shared, to the extent that we act intelligently in it, is *partly* of our creation. That is why we are responsible for those features of it that could be different were we to think and act otherwise. Whenever we accept a situation, after thinking about it in the light of its probable alternatives, we are not merely adjusting to it. For example, if a man accepts the present policy of preserving peace under "the balance of terror" as we grope toward multilateral disarmament, on the ground that this is the only viable alternative at present to surrender to Communism, which is the likely consequence of unilateral disarmament, or to a nuclear holocaust, he cannot be reasonably considered a standpatter.

The only person who is adjusted to his environment, in the mindless way Admiral Rickover implies, is one in a state of torpor, inattention, absence of interest, boredom. To be awake and alive in a world where problems exist means to be alarmed, on guard, ready to do something in relation to what is about to be or about to happen. Ironically, the pejorative educational connotations of "adjustment" may be most legitimately applied to the conceptions held by some of Dewey's critics.

In one of these connotations, adjustment suggests subordination to the status quo, not merely learning *about* the conditions of life but compliance with its norms. The "adjusted" individual assimilates social use and wont, the traditional ways of action, to the compulsions of natural necessity. In the past, education for this type of adjustment was associated with drill, habitual obedience, automatic response, the performance of set tasks under set conditions, the assumption that there is usually only one right way of doing anything and that some person in authority must ultimately define it. This kind of education is more reminiscent of traditional military training than of modern education.

An allied notion of "adjustment," as we have seen, is involved in views which regard the function of education to be the "pouring" or "cramming" of subject matter—honorifically labelled "the great traditions of the past"—into the students' minds, as if they were inert receptacles or containers to be filled rather than powers to be stirred and developed. Such an approach fails to give students a sense of *why* subject matters matter. It also fails to make ideas, people, and events come alive in the direct or imaginative experience of those who are learning.

All of these conceptions of adjustment or *self*-adjustment are foreign to Dewey's educational philosophy. For they do not envisage the adjustment of society to the moral imperatives of educational growth. Nor do they adjust the curriculum to the needs and capacities of students in order to achieve maximum educational growth. A curriculum designed and taught in the light of Dewey's philosophy seeks to quicken powers of perception, wherever relevant, into how things have become what they are; into how they may become better or worse; and into what our responsibility, personal or social, is for making them better or worse. It strives to make the student sensitive to the kind of problems he will have to meet in wider contexts when he is through with formal schooling. It is not romantic or utopian. Although it liberates the mind by opening visions of alternatives, it curbs the will and disciplines the imagination by recognizing that not all alternatives are possible or equally probable. Certain objective conditions must be learned and accepted in order to introduce intelligent changes. No one can be wise who is not resigned to something, or who tries to dissolve stubborn facts in the rose waters of myth or hope. But wherever conditions impinge upon men, men usually can also impinge upon conditions. One can adjust to the weather by letting oneself be rained on or by learning to keep dry in the rain. What is true of the weather is true of everything else that is meaningfully perceived in life—even death. So long as one remains conscious, one can determine something important about his own death. We can die like jackals or like men.

Terms like "adjustment" or "non-adjustment," like "conformism" or "non-conformism," are essentially relational. Used without reference to a context, as most critics employ them, they are meaningless. Unless we know *what* is being adjusted to and *how*, what is being conformed to or not, these terms have merely emotive overtones and no cognitive significance. When the context and use are supplied, the only kind of adjustment Dewey would approve of is that which follows the exercise of independent or creative intelligence and which does not create obstacles to its subsequent operation.

Before discussing the concepts of equality, democracy, and excellence in education, something should be said about the current emphasis upon "creativity" in education as if this were an independent element or goal in the process of education.

"Education for creativity" is an ambiguous phrase. No one can seriously maintain that the function of the schools is to find and develop creative persons as if this were a goal separate and distinct from developing critical persons or knowledgeable persons of educated sensibility. There can and should be special schools for those who give evidence of promise as creative artists or musicians. But the distinctive procedures of these schools obviously cannot be the procedures of the common or general school.

There is a sense in which "education for creativity" means little more than that the process of teaching should be a process of inquiry, kept ever fresh and interesting for the learner, by virtue of effective teaching techniques which draw him into the lesson as a participant in a common quest. Such teaching does not rely on rote learning or mechanical drill or threats or extrinsic rewards but on the perception of meaning. The development and enrichment of meanings require an intellectual discipline accepted as intrinsic to the proper execution of the task or problem.

There is a third sense in which "education for creativity" means that the school is to help the individual find himself in a

vocation or life pursuit which will call upon his special capacities and endowments. The insight, as old as Plato, that
most human beings find fulfillment in doing what they are
best qualified to do was not denied by Dewey. He insisted
only that individuals were developing creatures whose potentialities should not be typed too soon and that a type itself
is no more than a cluster of related differences. The aim of
education in a democratic society is personal growth; but
growth, to be significant, does not mean movement in all directions. The development of a mature human being is marked
not by a fitful succession of interests, but by the emergence
of an organizing center which gives purpose, direction, or
meaning to life. This is the role which Dewey once imagined
that vocations or callings would play in human experience
if ever a humane welfare economy replaced the market. We are
still far from the welfare economy he envisaged; but as we
have already seen, even if it is achieved there is little likelihood
that—except for a handful—it will provide significant vocational opportunities in which human beings can do creative
work. Science and technology have affected society more
pervasively than their optimistic prophets anticipated. In consequence, the problem of creativity in human life shifts from
the quest for creative callings—although there will always be
some callings of this character—to the creative use of leisure
in an automated society. It becomes the problem of developing the powers, the skills and inner resources which enable
human beings to live as persons in a most fruitful and satisfying
way. Today the electricians in the city of New York work
twenty-odd hours a week. Tomorrow they and their fellows
may work fewer. How will they spend the rest of the day?
The ideals of a liberal education reassert themselves at this
point. They should not be conceived as goals to be imposed
on the masses for tradition's sake but as opportunities for
liberation from the narrowing immediacies and synthetic ex-
citements by which the poor in spirit "kill time."

As I see it, the problem of creativity which must be faced

by education today is not the exploration of ways and means to make all individuals creative artists and thinkers, discoverers on the frontiers of knowledge. Biology defeats us here if we make this our primary goal. Nor is it merely the continuing task of developing inspiring and sympathetic teachers who can make learning enjoyable, not a chore or an assignment to be carried out to earn rewards or avoid penalties. This we must take for granted if we are serious about good teaching. We must conceive our educational task in the broadest sense. We must try to make it possible for as many individuals as we can reach through gifted teachers, using the best pedagogical methods available, to find and develop themselves as persons who can live with themselves and others, and who can enjoy in an active and participating way, on levels appropriate to their capacities, the goods and values of "ideal society"—literature, art, science, history, or any other ennobling interest or pursuit. These large aims may produce skeptical merriment among those who are convinced that a mass society inescapably must develop a cheap and shoddy mass culture which is essentially hostile to the high culture created and nurtured by an elite. Deploring the inanities and frivolities of mass culture as strongly as any, I am not convinced that they are a permanent feature of mass culture. Mass cultures as they exist in modern democratic societies are still young. The fact that high culture still continues to flourish in mass society, despite gloomy predictions that it would be destroyed by universal literacy and education, is not without its significance.

This theme trenches on the question of educational equality, democracy, and excellence.

The view that belief in "democracy in education" entails belief in equality, and that belief in equality leads to suspicion of diversity, and this in turn leads to hostility to the creative minority or elite, is held as an article of faith by prophets of the conservative educational revival. And since Dewey's philosophy is associated with this phrase, he is the object of much criticism as the alleged source of the levelling-down, the distrust of intelligence, the resentment against the gifted which presumably marks both American life and American education.

Before discussing Dewey's view on the meaning of equality in education, we might look a little closer at some of the indictments of American education on the score of its enmity to distinction, creativity, and ability. Most of them are not derived from any empirical study of behavior or value judgments but are on the level of a globe-trotter's impressions. The eminence of a writer in another field is no index to his competence to evaluate American education. In a discussion of the twin evils of conservatism and equalitarianism in American education, Arnold Toynbee writes that education has been crippled by a perverse notion of democracy which is characteristic of American society although not exclusive to it alone.

"This perverse notion is that to have been born with an exceptionally large endowment of innate ability is tantamount to having committed a large prenatal offence against society. It is looked upon as being an offence because, according to this wrong-headed view of democracy, inequalities of any and every kind are undemocratic. The gifted child is an offender . . ."[3] and more in this vein.

Mr. Toynbee's pronouncement is sucked out of his finger tips—a procedure for which, since he is talking about facts, he has even less justification than for his grandiose historical generalizations. Far from resenting inequalities of any and every kind or regarding them as undemocratic, popular culture in the United States shows too great a regard for some kinds of inequality—not merely regard for those who can make more money than others, which Toynbee recognizes, but too

[3] Arnold Toynbee: *The New York University Alumni News*, Vol. 7, No. 4. (January 1962), p. 3.

intense an admiration for outstanding skills in athletics or sports, for achievement in the cinema world, on the stage, in space travel from the early days of Lindbergh to Glenn. One can argue that not enough is done to identify and encourage the gifted child in American education despite the fact that progressive education at the outset, by stressing the importance of individual differences, made it easier to identify the gifted child. To maintain, however, that the gifted child, once identified, is resented, neglected where not hounded, and driven to acquire the mask of anonymity and mediocrity in order to remain at peace with his less gifted fellows, is an entirely different proposition—and one for which there is no evidence. It simply is not the case that democracy in the United States either in theory or in practice is hostile to the recognition of differences in achievement and distinction, whether in crime or in music. The very worship of "the bitch goddess Success" in every field, whether material, professional, or academic, testifies to an appreciation of differences in talent and achievement. Toynbee charges that the great premium which American public opinion places on "social conformity" is a consequence of the educational policy of "egalitarianism in childhood." But he misconceives the meaning of "democracy in education" both as presented in the writings of its chief protagonists and in the fumbling efforts of American educational practice to realize it.

To clarify some of the important distinctions we can hardly do better than to restate what "democracy in education" means in the educational writings of John Dewey and its bearing on current practices.

The essence of Dewey's view is that democracy is committed to an equality of concern for each individual in the community to develop himself as a person. Education is the chief means by which those personal capacities are to be discovered and liberated. Education should enable human beings to achieve their maximum *distinctive* growth in harmony with their fellows. Equality of concern is not the same thing as equal treatment. It is compatible with unequal treatment, provided this treatment is required by the necessities of intellectual and emotional growth in each case. "Moral equality," he says, "means incommensurability, the inapplicability of common and quantitative standards. It means intrinsic qualities which require *unique* opportunities and *differential* manifestation . . ." The principle of moral equality or ideal democracy is the most revolutionary principle in the world because its scope embraces all social institutions.

Even a half-careful reading of Dewey reveals that individuals for him come first in the order of concern, and that to be an individual is to be different in some distinctive and important way from others even though many things are shared in common with others. Conceptually, it is very difficult to express this union of equality of concern with difference of treatment in a formal rule. But we may illustrate it by reference to another institution. In a healthy and happy family where children vary in age, strength, and intellectual gifts, it would be absurd for parents to treat them equally in specific situations—absurd precisely because they are considered equally, valued equally. A family, of course, cannot be taken as a literal model for a complex society—there are no parents in society—but ethically it illustrates the principle which Dewey believed should be exhibited in the functioning of social institutions in a democracy, or which should be its controlling and guiding spirit. And it is striking to observe how often Dewey uses the family for analogical purposes to make an educational recommendation. Consider, for example, his well-known words: "What the best and wisest parent wants for his own child, that must the community want for all its children. Any other ideal for our schools is narrow and unlovely; acted upon, it destroys our democracy."

The significance of this observation is all the more important as an indicator of Dewey's meaning because the words are such an obvious overstatement. We have never acted on this ideal and have not destroyed our democracy, because democracy so conceived has never really existed. But these words do express in the most emphatic way an entire complex of values, values which must guide our action if we are to approach closer to the democratic ideal. And this ideal rests on the primacy of freedom, on the right to be different, on the right to be an individual—so much so that, although social institutions are recognized as the indispensable means by which personality is aided in coming to development, all social institutions must nevertheless be criticized and reformed in the light of the qualities of human experience to which they give rise. The individual person comes first in the order of significance, not of time.

The educational corollaries which follow from such a democratic philosophy are fantastically different from those drawn by critics who see in it the prolegomenon to an ideological justification for mediocrity. The very contrary is true. Mediocrity is the consequence of imposing one uniform pattern on individual differences, of the attempt to make everyone talk and sing and think alike about the same things at the same time. How can Dewey's philosophy be interpreted as advocating that the gifted child be denied the special attention which would bring his gifts to fruition? Historically, the earliest concern with providing appropriate educational opportunities for gifted children was manifested by educators and psychologists strongly influenced by Dewey. By all means, education must aim at excellence! But is there only one kind of excellence? Must one excellence be sacrificed to another? Must, as Ernest Renan asks, whatever is unfit for the altar of the gods be thrown to the dogs? Or, put more concretely, does it follow that, because we should exert our efforts to provide the educational stimulation that will generate the most fruitful results for students of the highest IQ, we should therefore not exert ourselves to generate the most fruitful results for students of lower IQs? If this is what it means, where is our equality of concern?

We must distinguish between standards of achievement that individuals must meet before certain professions are open to them—and from which, both in their own personal interests and in those of society, they can be legitimately barred—and the standard of growth and progress that is applicable to each individual. It is the latter which concerns the teacher, insofar as he accepts responsibility for the education of the person. And this means not the elimination or the dilution of subject matter, not the substitution of play for study, not a cafeteria of snap courses—but holding up ever higher goals to be reached by every student until he has attained *his* best. Such an approach is perfectly compatible with prescribed courses and studies. For if all needs are individual, many of them are at the same time common needs in a common world of common dangers and opportunities. There are some things everyone needs to know. Not everything, however, needs to be known by everybody.

What this democratic conception of education involves is better grasped by contrasting it with the view that would discriminate not merely *between* capacities but *against* them. Such a view advocates a kind of elite system in which the prizes and the power are to go to those who by natural endowment or social preferment (the two are often hard to separate) reach the head of their class. It not only differentiates but subtly demeans, by suggesting that the hierarchy of intelligence is the key to the hierarchy of human value, and that this hierarchy sooner or later determines position in a hierarchy of social standing and political power. Sometimes this view also calls itself democratic, but its spirit as well as its recommendations are altogether opposed to democracy as Dewey understood it.

Let us examine, for example, the view of Professor William Hocking, who has written widely on education. For him genuine democracy consists in *"the democracy of identical standard"* to be applied to all, irrespective of capacities. And he explains his meaning by an analogy: "We do not, in our athletic contests, trim the length of the mile to the convenience of the runners: The democracy of the race does not consist in the assumption that everybody must get a prize; it consists in the identity of the spacing and timing for all entrants. This is what democracy must mean in higher education, and to retain this integrity, there must be losers, and a thinning out of the mass trend to the colleges."[4] What this means in practice is indicated by the question: "But where is the college which is willing to flunk 50 per cent of its graduating class?"

Hocking does not explain why democracy means this only in higher education and not in secondary or even primary education. If "every man has a right and duty to be a whole man," as he puts it, why has not every individual a right to that kind of education which will carry him further to that wholeness at any level? And what has all this to do with degress or certification of professional competence, which are fundamentally socially protective devices? And above all, what has the process of education to do with a race? And even in a race, we do not expect, unless we are Nietzschean, the halt, the blind, the crippled to start from scratch. And if the course of study is to be considered a race course, who ever heard of fifty per cent of the runners winning the prize? Why not flunk ninety per cent of the graduating class—indeed, why not all except the man who wins by coming in first?

The analogy reveals the unconscious, anti-democratic, almost Prussian conception underlying this view of education. Education is not a race or a combat or a competition, although, properly implemented, these may be pedagogic devices to add zest to learning. If we must use language of this sort, it is better to have the individual run a race against his own potentialities;

[4] William Hocking: *Experiment in Education* (Chicago: Henry Regnery Co.; 1954), p. 275.

which means, since they grow with achievement, that the race, like the process of education and self-education, is never finished.

Allied to the conception of education as the process by which prizes and power are won is the view of society as a graded and hierarchically organized system, in which intelligence—not birth, social status, or wealth—is the principle of differentiation. No matter what the principle of differentiation is, if it involves hierarchy, official or unofficial, it involves the likelihood of exploitation. It is well to realize that we do not owe the great movements for social justice and political freedom to the educated classes of hierarchically ordered European societies. On the whole, these classes sided with church and king and the social status quo during the centuries of struggle for the extension of human rights. Higher intelligence and specialized education give both the duty and right to exercise specific functions in a complex society, but so does not-so-high intelligence and more general education. Unless there is a mutuality of esteem and a recognition that there are many kinds of desirable distinctions, the entire principle of distinction becomes invidious, a badge of social snobbery and an instrument by which special interests are furthered. A society in which there are class struggles between the better educated and the less well educated, between the more intelligent and the less intelligent, not only violates the principles of moral equality, but is one in which the best educated are likely to lose.

There is another aspect of democracy in education which is intimately connected with modern American education. It has been travestied and caricatured not only by critics, but by some unintelligent followers of Dewey. This is the view that at appropriate levels the student's educational experience—his group meetings, school projects, class organization—should exhibit some of the values which are central to the ethics of democracy. In a country of different races and varied ethnic groups, in which the family itself may be the original breeding place of violent prejudice, such activities are all the more necessary. Whatever "character education" is, it is more likely to be effective by being lived than by being preached. Where students are made responsible for some aspects of their school life, this need not interfere either with the time devoted to learning or with the seriousness with which learning is prosecuted. A skillful teacher can so organize instruction that often the educational lesson or project draws all children into it in some participating role for which they take responsibility.

The easiest way to make this idea ridiculous is to try to carry it out with young toughs or hooligans produced by the breakdown of family and community life in large cities—especially where there has been a recent influx of immigrants. A pinch of common sense is sometimes better than a carload of speculative pedagogy. Although Dewey never realized the extent and gravity of the problem, he did recognize that in the case of disturbed and unruly students who "stand permanently in the way of the educational activities of others . . . exclusion is perhaps the *only* available measure at a *given* juncture, even though it is no solution." (Italics mine.)

Every classroom teacher knows that it requires only one or two such students to make genuine teaching impossible. Nonetheless, the community—or rather, newspapers and educational pressure groups which decry modern education—cites the existence of such elements (which in the past either did not get to school or received short shrift when they did) as evidence of the failure of modern education. Nothing in Dewey's or anybody else's educational philosophy requires the schools to function like psychiatric and/or police institutions. *Something should and can be done for such students*—a democratic society should be equally concerned about them, too, but they must be firmly excluded for their sake and the sake of other children from the normal school environment until they are rehabilitated in special educational schools. We must realize the heavy responsibility of the community in failing to provide the kind of social environment and conditions which are the birthright of all children in a society which professes to be democratic. Nonetheless it is wrong to visit the sins of the fathers upon their offspring in education or anywhere else. Disease, too, has its social origins and conditions but tubercular children require the tender care of a sanitarium and not the run of a classroom of normal children. If we permit sentimentalism to drive out common sense in facing the difficult problems of discipline in some large metropolitan centers, we invite a return to the worst features of the worst days of the "blackboard jungle." Our choice is not limited to the doctrinaire permissiveness of the sentimentalist in education and the despotic authoritarianism of the traditionalist for whom the rod is as important as the book in education.

Some cautionary words are in order about the concern for "excellence in education" which so stcongly marks recent literature. There is a danger that unless presented with specific curricular programs, it may become only another phrase or slogan. When everyone mouths the same formula, including those who only yesterday had been arrayed against each other in fierce controversy, it is likely that different things are intended by it. First of all, it should be recognized that as an educational ideal, the pursuit of excellence is perfectly compatible with stress on equality of educational opportunity. If we are sincerely committed to encouraging excellence of achievement for our entire school population, we must, so to speak, discourage the presence of all the invidious distinctions —racial, religious, political, economic—which prevent those capable of profiting from the highest reaches of education from realizing their talents. This means, as a corollary, the readiness to underwrite by a system of scholarships the higher education of every talented student, for the community's benefit as well as his own. Yet some of the most vocal advocates of educational excellence are wedded to economic dogmas which oppose measures of this sort by the government. Second, we must not identify some types of educational excellence, for which there is a pressing, and perhaps only transitory, social need, with excellence as such. As we have already maintained, emphasis upon them may be justifiable but it should not blind us to the existence of multiple forms of excellence. Third, we should be wary against converting our appreciation of excellence into a *cult*, as if only the excellent is important and nothing else counts. If the term means anything, we cannot all be excellent. But in education we can all do better than we have done.

In the intellectual history of the West, the cult of excellence has sometimes been associated with an ideology which disdains equal social, political, and, sometimes human rights of those who are less than excellent. There is an entire family of doctrines which assume that a cultural and educational elite should function as a political and ruling elite. This confuses different issues, especially when occasional words of the great democratic spokesmen of the past are cited in support of the position. The upper ranges of any normal distribution of talent in any field may be referred as an elite. In this sense, to say that there is a natural aristocracy of talent, on the basis of current biological theory, is a commonplace. Every adequate educational system—which to a democrat means one in which equality of opportunity prevails—ought to enable us to discover this natural aristocracy of talent. But to couple a natural aristocracy of talent with a natural aristocracy of virtue, as Jefferson did in a letter to John Adams, is questionable, and to suggest that both are "the most precious gift of nature for the instruction, the trusts and government of society," is to invite misunderstanding of the democratic ethos. The few references in Jefferson to the natural aristocracy of talent and *virtue*, as well as his contemptuous reference to those who are not part of the aristocracy, when speaking of the select few who "will be raked from the rubbish annually" and educated at public expense for higher study, are decidedly unrepresentative of the character of his basic democratic faith. They can no more be taken as indicative of his whole, considered view than can his *jeu d'esprit* that a little bloodletting every twenty years is good for the health of a democracy.

In a democracy we can have education for expertness of any kind, including education for civil service officials as well as generals and physicians. We cannot, strictly speaking, have education for political leadership, as distinct from the political education of all the citizens of the community. It was the political education of the whole people that Jefferson was most concerned with, of a kind that would immunize them against the usurpations of power. This squares with his reiterated belief that political freedom "can never be safe except in the hands of the people themselves," rather than in any aristocracy of talent or virtue, and that ultimate political authority must rest with them. This faith may be mistaken but without it there can be no reasoned defense of democracy. Nonetheless Jefferson was aware that to entrust political power to the people was not a sufficient guarantee of the perpetuation of political freedom. Without proper education, a people could not long remain free. The abiding political function of education in a democracy, therefore, is to impart the knowledge, develop the skills, and strengthen the values which are required to enable men to make a success of the experiment of self-government. Everything else is a matter of relative curricular detail for him in this respect.

The picture of the contemporary educational scene would be incomplete if it made no mention of the impact of the methods of analytic philosophy upon theorizing, or more accurately, writing about education. From one point of view this development is to be welcomed. There is an extraordinary amount of looseness in educational writing, which goes beyond the vagueness necessarily entailed by the use of large and undefined concepts like "life," "experience," and "education." This looseness interferes with proper communication and often prevents participants in heated debate from focusing on pertinent problems or even understanding what the genuine arguments or disagreements are. Definitions in use are sometimes confused with personal resolutions or stipulations to give familiar words new meanings, and both with disguised statements of fact or evaluation. Different types of relationships between ideas and ideas, ideas and men, and ideas and social movements are obscured by blanket terms. Influences on educational theory and practice are ascribed to philosophical ideas and systems in ways which will not stand critical examination for a moment. A greater attention to context and usage, an effort to state things with definiteness if not with precision, could banish from educational writing much of the nebulosity and soapiness which afflict it.

To the extent that the techniques of analytic philosophy are able to achieve this result, their appearance in articles and books concerned with education can do only good. Unfortunately, the few writings which have so far appeared by educators inspired by the linguistic approach, with rare exceptions, have not been conspicuous for the light they have shed on educational issues of importance. Some have merely added an additional stratum of linguistic obscurity created by the multiplication of verbal distinctions which make no objective difference to the understanding or resolution of any specific educational problems.

The whole approach of the analytic method, or the movement of linguistic analysis, as currently applied to the theory and practice of education, seems to me to be largely misconceived. For it takes its point of departure not from specific problems of teaching and learning, of educational goals and curriculum-making, but from the *language* employed by educators without further reference to educational practice or the problematic situations which presumably are the matrix of educational concern.

The consequence of trying to illumine the educational process by linguistic analysis sometimes leads to bizarre conclusions. One practitioner of this technique comes to the conclusion that "properly speaking" to have an education is to believe what one has been taught, and to be properly taught a belief requires that sentences expressing it be uttered by the teacher before the learner can acquire the belief. I call this conclusion bizarre because, although some kinds of didactic instruction are covered by this analysis, it omits an enormous range of objectives normally taken as proper subjects of instruction—skills, habits, and attitudes. More important, it fails to do justice to the most valuable kinds of teaching in which students discover truths for themselves. A good teacher can so organize the materials of instruction that students are led to the belief that "the earth is round" without the teacher's needing to utter the statement. Because ordinary language is vague and, without reference to specific context, ambiguous, proposals about how we should talk about education, or use the language of education, might be helpful in clarifying conflicting and obscure usage. But for educators, even this is of peripheral interest unless it can be brought to bear at some point on the processes of teaching and learning and the problems arising therefrom.

Analysis of terms like "knowing," "learning," "teaching," "education," and their cognate expressions, when not controlled by their specific contexts, is apt to be too vague, general, and misleading because each one of them embraces a whole family of notions. Linguistic analysis can usefully distinguish the various senses and contexts in which these terms are used. Its upshot at best will be a classification of actual and possible usages and their relationships. What is not so clear is the bearing this linguistic analysis has on *educational* problems. What is sometimes referred to as the relevance or implication of linguistic analysis for education turns out to be no more than a reference to certain educational expressions which illustrate the analysis. That is to say, when we ask for the bearing of the analysis on educational theory and practice, we are not referred to any specific educational problem which serves as the controlling point of departure, but to certain ways of speaking or writing by educators which illustrate distinctions made by the analysis. But in view of the large claims made for the linguistic-analysis approach, it is pertinent to ask: what can educators learn from it in their specifically professional interests? What decisions of *what* to teach, *how* to teach, *whom* to teach, *when* to teach, or even answers to *why* teach, depend on the upshot of linguistic analysis? Whether 'knowing that" sentences are or are not reducible to "knowing how" sentences, or whether we should or should not propose certain usages in the language of education as "legislative," is relevant to problems of teaching and learning only if it can be shown that some existing confusion in the theory or practice of education is cleared up by the analysis or if it purifies or extends or challenges an insight, suggests or reveals some error of omission or commission. No teacher needs the benefit of linguistic analysis to realize that a child may learn to answer questions on the duties of a good citizen correctly yet habitually disregard them or that he may be scrupulously honest yet not know in what honesty consists; that knowing how to spell a word is not the same as knowing what it means or that it has a meaning at all. To deny these truisms would be comparable to denying that a person can sing without knowing the scales or the rules of composition, a denial that would reveal one as beyond the help of any kind of analysis.

Some discussions which are offered as illustrations of linguistic analysis in education seem to ignore the common-sense presuppositions of ordinary language. They triumphantly reject as absurd or meaningless certain expressions in use, by disregarding their obvious contexts and hypnotically fixing on the form and words of the sentence. They apparently regard this procedure as evidencing the relevance of analysis for education. A particularly crass instance of this is found in some recent analyses of one of the key injunctions of modern education: "Teach the child, not the subject." Anyone who observes the context of this injunction understands it to mean: "Teach the subject with primary reference to the child's capacities and needs" or "Teach the subject so that it becomes a meaningful experience to the child" or "Teach the child, and not merely the subject." This injunction may be reasonably defended or rejected on the ground of the consequences of acting on it compared with other teaching procedures, and in the light of the values we place on the growth of personality, the mastery of subject matter, and similar considerations. Its truth or falsity is of momentous importance. Not so to some writers who make short shrift of it with one analytical swoop. It doesn't even qualify to be considered. One writer maintains that assertions like " 'teach the child, not content' are ludicrous when cast in the role of generalizations . . . because the notion of teaching someone without teaching him something is nonsense." Alas this makes nonsense of the complaint that some students (and many parents) have made of teachers that "they have taught us (or them) nothing." This is impossible by definition! The retort to this is obvious. One cannot dispose of an empirical question by linguistic analysis. What the modern educator is saying is that the teacher has failed to teach his subject success-fully because of his disregard of the needs of the learner. The point of saying that "the teacher has taught us nothing" is that "we have learned nothing because of his failure to relate what he was trying to teach to our background of knowledge, our readiness, our level of intelligence, etc."

Another writer of the same school asserts: "The statement 'I teach children, not subject matter' is absurd," because "teach-ing is a triadic relation, that is someone (a teacher) teaches something (subject-matter) to someone (a student)." If we were to read this last statement with the same absent-minded-ness with which its author reads the statement *he* finds absurd, we would have to conclude that it is equally absurd to say that a man can teach himself or that he can learn a lesson from nature or hundreds of other sensible things. This kind of analysis is comparable to dismissing the claim of a dictator, "The State is I," as meaningless, as an obvious category mistake since a person cannot be an organization. What should really be obvious is that this assertion is extremely meaningful; every intelligent person knows what to expect when he hears it and what is being denied by it.

Not all efforts of linguistic analysis in education lead to such results. But all too often they leave an impression comparable to that produced by someone who, having failed to grasp the point of a joke which everyone else has enjoyed, tries to prove by strict analysis that the joke really has no point, something even more depressing than trying to explain it. We must be on guard lest linguistic analysis, which at its best helps us to express things in a way that leads to greater self-understanding or to readier inquiry and test, surreptitiously commits us to conclusions on facts or policies which cannot be reached by analysis alone but primarily through the warrants of empirical investigation.

Linguistic analysis, if it is not exercised independently of our ordinary mother-wit and common sense, can uncover assumptions we make of which we are unaware. It can show without difficulty that discussions of knowing and learning in education offered as paradigms are not usually comprehensive or inclusive enough, that they do not do justice to all the activities which have been designated as such in ordinary speech, and that an implicit value-assumption controls the discussion. The assumption is that the paradigmatic analysis holds not for everything which goes by the name of knowing, teaching, or learning but only for some selected or preferred type usually called "genuine," "real," or "most significant." An issue of an entirely different order from the question of the adequacy of the analysis of the processes of teaching and learning arises when we face the challenge to justify the claim that one or another mode of teaching and learning is of greater worth or fruitfulness.

This is the crucial point which concerns the "philosophy of education." Many are the subjects discussed under the rubric of philosophy of education and many the varieties of discourse in which these discussions are couched. All of them are easily accommodated under more or less well defined disciplines like psychology, sociology, comparative government, and anthropology. The only distinctive theme with which the philosophy of education has concerned itself from Plato to Dewey is: what should the aims or goals of education be? This is a normative problem and is inescapable once the existing aims of an educational system are challenged or put in doubt. It cuts deep and involves at some point complex problems of the methods as well as the content of education; for any answer to the normative question concerning what basic values should inform and direct the entire educational enterprise presupposes a theory of human nature, a conception of what man is and may become. Thousands of massive facts about human biology and history, social organization and economy bear upon the options open to us. A wise decision will take note of them. It may even give them a certain veto power. But in the end the goals we lay down as fundamental for education will embody our conceptions of the reasonable and desirable, what we hope as well as what we know. When Dewey, for example, stresses the fact that "there is no such thing as genuine knowledge and fruitful understanding except as the offspring of (experimental) *doing*," he is making assertions not only about the different kinds of knowledge individuals may acquire and how they acquire it, but about the worth and desirability of an education whose best illustrations of the processes of learning are drawn from the laboratory rather than the seminary.

Men received an education long before philosophers of education appeared on the scene. They acquired knowledge and used methods in accordance with custom and tradition, slowly adopting modifications to further inherited purposes. New inventions and discoveries, wars, revolutions, and less dramatic social changes affected both the methods and the content of education and gave rise to explicit challenges to accepted ideals. To the extent that these challenges are recognized and accepted or rejected, philosophies of education come to life. The view that a philosophy of education represents merely an application to the process of education of philosophical truths antecedently won is demonstrably false for most philosophies of education; when true, it indicates their superficiality and irrelevance to actual educational concern. A philosophy of education must grow out of live issues in situations marked by doubt, disagreement, or conflict and should not be tested by reference to values and goals imposed upon education from without. If these values and goals have validity, they can establish themselves in the thick of educational experience. It would be truer to say that a general philosophy is likely to have more to recommend it if its principal positions have emerged as a consequence of reflection on value conflicts in education, law, economics, and other subject matters. A philosophy renders itself ridiculous if, on the strength of its conception of truth, it tries to dictate or correct the deliverances of controlled experiment, whether in physics or the psychology of learning or the psychology of reading. On the contrary, the test of the validity of its theory is its adequacy to the truths we live by and the new truths won by pushing back the frontiers of knowledge. From this point of view, any conception of truth which condemns *all* claims to human knowledge as badly mistaken or infected with radical skepticism condemns itself.

An adequate philosophy of education will never ignore empirical practices including the ways in which we speak of them. But it must illumine the empirical scene from a large human perspective. That is why without some synoptic visions of the paths open to men in their quest for a desirable society, without a vital concern for the human condition in this place and in this time, a purely linguistic approach to educational problems is barren. It does not even reach the plane of a philosophy of education.

What is required of a philosophy of education today is the development in the context of educational theory and practice of a viable set of values for an age of brilliant experimental advance and threatening social regression. The triumphs of experimental science in our age have been accompanied by the complete eclipse of freedom in some areas and grave threats to its continued existence in those centers in which, however imperfect, free institutions have enjoyed wide sway.

Consequently, an adequate philosophy of education today will not only reflect the social order in which it arises but will also serve to criticize and redirect it. Civilizations may be evaluated from many points of view. None can lead to more fruitful and satisfying results than an educational point of view which recognizes and cherishes diversity of interests and personality, lavishes an equality of concern upon their cultivation, and aims at excellence of achievement in whatever the human brain or hand turns to. If freedom is to have a future, our philosophy of education must help sustain a passion for it by the arts of intelligence and imagination.

Chapter 2

THE ENDS OF EDUCATION

"It is true that the aim of education is development of individuals to the utmost of their potentialities. But this statement in isolation leaves unanswered the question as to what is the measure of the development. A society of free individuals in which all, through their own work, contribute to the liberation and enrichment of the lives of others, is the only environment in which any individual can really grow normally to his full stature."

JOHN DEWEY

EVERYONE who makes an intelligent educational decision—whether as student, teacher, parent, or citizen—must sooner or later be able to justify it by reference to what he conceives the ends of education to be. These ends do not alone determine what should be done, but without them action has no focus. It is a matter of form, of imitation or routine.

Where the ends of education are explicitly stated, as they often are in current discussion, there seems to be a wide agreement about them. Differences appear just as soon as we ask about ends the same question we asked about decisions: How are *they* derived and justified? Similarly, there is more agreement about the phrasing of the ends of education than about their concrete meaning in any specific cultural context. I shall try to show that conflicting interpretations of the meaning of educational ends are significantly associated with the different ways in which these ends are derived and applied.

It is not difficult to draw up a list of educational ends to which most educators who are not open apologists for a political or religious church will subscribe independently of their philosophical allegiance.

(1) Education should aim to develop the powers of critical, independent thought.

(2) It should attempt to induce sensitiveness of perception, receptiveness to new ideas, imaginative sympathy with the experiences of others.

(3) It should produce an awareness of the main streams of our cultural, literary, and scientific traditions.

(4) It should make available important bodies of knowledge concerning nature, society, ourselves, our country, and its history.

(5) It should strive to cultivate an intelligent loyalty to the ideals of the democratic community and to deepen understanding of the heritage of freedom and the prospects of its survival.

(6) At some level, it should equip young men and women with the general skills and techniques and the specialized knowledge which, together with the virtues and aptitudes already mentioned, will make it possible for them to do some productive work related to their capacities and interests.

(7) It should strengthen those inner resources and traits of character which enable the individual, when necessary, to stand alone.

Not only can the seven liberal arts in their modern version be derived from these ends, but we can take them collectively as defining the aim of a liberal education. Any individual in whom the qualities and capacities necessary to achieve these ends have been liberated has received a liberal education. Why, then, should controversy be so rife? After all, if these ends of education are granted, it should not be an insuperable task to decide which specific course of study in a determinate time and place will best realize them. Yet despite the enormous amount of experimental data compiled by educational psychologists, the conflict of schools and philosophies continues unabated. If anything, it has grown more bitter in recent years.

The situation is not unique in education. In the realm of morals, too, we can observe precisely the same thing. Everyone believes, or says he believes, in truth, justice, loyalty, honor, dignity. Yet the strife of moral systems and the diversity of moral judgments in concrete situations, where the same formal values are invoked, is even more conspicuous than in education. In part, the same reason accounts for differences in both moral and educational judgments. Values or goods are plural in morals, just as ends in education are plural. They conflict not only with the values, goods, and ends that are rejected but to some extent among themselves. Two parties to a dispute may both profess allegiance to the ideals of justice *and* happiness or to the goods of security *and* adventure. But they may evaluate them differently, and assign them different weights when faced by the necessity of choice. Similarly, although different schools of education subscribe to critical intelligence *and* loyalty, natural piety for one's traditions *and* independent exploration of new modes of thought, they may be worlds apart in their practical judgments because they accent differently the values they hold in common. They can reach a consensus only insofar as they both submit to a *common method* of resolving conflicts of value in specific situations. But it is at the point of method, i.e., the process by which ideals are themselves derived and evaluated, that they fundamentally divide.

There is another basic reason why the profession of common ends in a common situation is no assurance of agreement. The same words may actually mean different things to those who use them. Anyone who has read Hitler's *Mein Kampf* will find that he invokes many of the ideals of his democratic opponents. He talks about justice, honesty, dignity, craftsmanship, discipline, and willingness to sacrifice. In one passage he asserts that "the importance of the Person" is the distinguishing character-istic of the Nazi philosophy of life which "therefore makes the individual the pillar of the entire edifice."[1] The terms "reason," "freedom," "order," and "discipline" appear in the writings of neo-Thomists, absolute idealists, and experimental naturalists. But they do not mean the same thing. Were one to judge educators only by their *language* in discussing ultimate educational goals, there would be little ground for suspecting the presence of profound differences among them. The situa-tion is closely analogous in political philosophy. Do not all political groups in this country declare their staunch support of the ideals expressed in the Declaration of Independence? Who does not *call* himself a democrat these days? Even Fascists and Communists adorn the chains by which they bind the bodies and spirits of their subjects with flowers of demo-cratic rhetoric.

How, then, do we know when those who accept the same ideals have a common referent or meaning? Roughly, only when these words are conjoined with, or lead to, common be-havior or a program of action culminating in common behav-ior, in a series of common historical situations. This is the prescript of crude common sense as well as of refined scientific method. Indeed, we sometimes come to the conclusion that despite the use of different words people mean the same thing because the programs and behavior to which the words lead are virtually identical. No understanding between human beings is possible without symbols; but the symbols do not have to be verbal. Although it would be extremely difficult, in prin-ciple it would not be impossible for human beings to under-stand each other—on a rather primitive level to be sure—if they could not employ words. But without reference to some kind of co-operative bodily behavior, actual or prospective, remem-

[1] Adolf Hitler: *Mein Kampf* (English ed.; New York: Reynal and Hitchcock; 1949), p. 668.

bered or imagined, no matter how long we spoke with one another there would be no assurance of mutual understanding. Even gods and angels have to intrude in the natural order to communicate with men.

The concrete application of these observations to educational ends is twofold. The function of these general ends is not to serve as a rhetorical prologue to programs of education —which is their purpose in the catalogues of most liberal arts colleges—but, first, to suggest a multiplicity of specific ends in the details of instruction. There should be an intimate relation between the objectives of different studies and the underlying ends. Second, these ends must interpenetrate the methods and means of instruction. Nothing is more familiar than the disparity between professed goals and daily practice. Educational ideals operate only insofar as they are continuous with *what* subjects are studied and *how* they are studied. Their true meaning becomes apparent in educational practices and institutions. When these change, the meaning of the ideals changes even when the same words are retained. A hypnotic fixation on words or labels alone creates an insensitiveness, and sometimes an indifference, to the varied contents they conceal.

The most general aims of institutional education in any community are identical with the most general aims of moral (or immoral) action in that community. When we disapprove of the aims of an educational system, and state what they *should* be, we are also indicating, to the extent that they are educationally relevant, what the aims of the good life should be. How, then, do we determine what the aims of education or the good life should be?

There are two generic ways of reaching what are sometimes called "the ultimate" ends of education. One relies on an immediate, self-certifying *intuition* of the nature of man; the other on the observation of the consequences of different proposals of treating man. The first is essentially theological and metaphysical; the second is experimental and scientific.

When they are intelligently formulated both approaches recognize that the ends of education are relevant to the nature of man. But a world of difference separates their conception of the nature of man. The religious or metaphysical approach seeks to deduce what men *should be* from what they *are*. And what they are can only be grasped by an intuition of their "essential" nature. Whatever the differences between Aristotle, Aquinas, and Rousseau on other points—and they are vast—all assert that from the true nature of man the true nature of education follows logically. If we know what man is, then we can lay down the essentials of an adequate education for all men, everywhere, always. The scientific approach, on the other hand, is interested in discovering what the nature of man is, not in terms of an absolute essence, but *in terms of a developing career in time* and in relation to the world of things, culture, and history of which he is an inseparable part. It recognizes man's nature not as a premise from which to deduce the aims of education, but as a set of *conditions* which limit the range of *possible* educational aims in order to select the best or most *desirable* from among those for which man's nature provides a ground. An education should not be what it cannot be; it can be what it should not be; it may be what it should be.

In this chapter I shall briefly indicate an experimental approach to the question of educational ends and their relation to human nature. In the next, I shall consider the opposing claims made for a currently fashionable metaphysical view.

There are at least three distinguishable, but not separable, aspects of man's nature that are relevant to the formulation of valid educational ideals. (a) First, man is a biological organism subject to definite laws of growth. Certain powers and capacities mature, flourish, and decline according to a definite cycle. (b) Second, man is a member of society, heir to a cultural heritage and social organization that determine the forms in which his biological needs and impulses find expression. (c) Third, man as a personality or character exhibits a distinctive pattern of behavior, rooted in biological variation and influenced by the dominant norms of his culture, which he gradually develops through a series of successive choices.

Given these threefold aspects of man's powers, what ends of education should be stressed, and why? We say ends, rather than end, because an education that is relevant to at least these three aspects of human nature will have plural, even if related, ends.

(a) In relation to the development of the human organism, physical and mental, a desirable education takes as its end *growth*. By "growth" I mean the maturation of man's natural powers toward the highest desirable point which his body, his mind, and his culture make possible. It is a process which results physically in a state of health, and intellectually in a continuing activity of self-education.

The maturation of body and mind is natural; but so is stunting and retardation. Therefore, in selecting growth as an end, we are not *deducing* what should be from what is but are choosing the preferred consequences of one mode of action rather than another. There are many societies in which the development of certain features of the body and powers of the mind is not encouraged. For the same reason, since there are multiple possibilities of development, in selecting growth we are selecting a certain type or kind of development.

Growth, as everyone knows, has been emphasized by John Dewey as one of the central aims of education. But, as soon as one speaks of growth, critics who approach this end as if it were being urged in isolation from others are sure to inquire: growth in what direction? There is criminal growth, fascist growth, cancerous growth. From the fact that a thing is, it doesn't follow that it must or should grow. From the belief that a thing should grow, we do not yet know what direction the potentialities of growth should be encouraged to take. The necessity for a social frame of reference is clearly indicated as soon as we select growth as an educational end.

No one has seen this more clearly nor stressed it more insistently than John Dewey. From the very outset the end of personal growth has been allied with the social end of democracy in his educational philosophy. "This idea [that the object and reward of learning is continued capacity for growth] cannot be applied to *all* the members of a society except where intercourse of man with man is mutual, and except where there is adequate provision for the reconstruction of social habits and institutions by means of wide stimulation arising from equitably distributed interests. And this means a democratic society."[2]

Education for growth, then, goes hand in hand with education for democracy and a justification of one is tantamount to a justification of the other. But why continuous growth even if democracy is accepted as a social goal? There are at least two reasons. One flows from the nature of the democratic ideal, which is incompatible with fixed social divisions. It cannot function properly where individuals are trained independently of their maturing powers and possibilities of development. The second is that a world in which continuous growth is encouraged is more likely to make for the diversification and enrichment of experience than a world where individuals remain at the same level they have reached at the close of their schooling, learning nothing new even if they forget nothing old.

(b) We have already seen that every choice we make in selecting and fortifying certain tendencies among the plurality of potentialities in the individual must be undertaken from the standpoint of some social philosophy, or some ideal of social organization. What, then, are the grounds for our choice of the democratic social philosophy? Here, also, as in the case of the justification of ends, there are two generic approaches open to those who recognize the validity of the question—a metaphysical or religious "demonstration" ultimately based

[2] John Dewey: *Democracy and Education* (New York: The Macmillan Company; 1916), p. 117.

on absolute intuitions, and an empirical approach which regards the test of consequences as decisive.

The metaphysical and theological premises from which the validity of democracy has been allegedly derived are of the most heterogeneous variety. Many of them are mutually incompatible. They have been offered by polytheists, monotheists, atheists; Jews, Mohammedans, and Christians; Catholics, Lutherans, and Unitarians; and by philosophers of diverse schools. This suggests that the conviction with which the democratic ideal is held rests not so much on alleged metaphysical presuppositions that are beyond the test of experience, but on the actual or anticipated values of democracy in experience as contrasted with nondemocratic alternatives. It is interesting to observe that these *nondemocratic* alternatives historically have been justified by the identical metaphysical and theological presuppositions which have been advanced as the alleged premises on which democracy rests. And since these premises are compatible with social philosophies that are mutually contradictory, the latter cannot be derived from the former.

The existence of democratic communities in which individuals of conflicting religious faiths and metaphysical beliefs sincerely co-operate in democracy's support indicates that it is possible to find criteria for accepting democracy that do not depend on revelation or intuition. Indeed, to claim that democracy is uniquely entailed by only one set of theological or metaphysical intuitions, and that no one can sincerely or consistently be a democrat who does not embrace them, is not only logically false—it imperils the very existence of a democratic community. For the nonempirical character of these intuitions makes it impossible to find a workable method by which conflicts among them may be resolved and uncoerced agreements reached. In matters of faith, each sect regards itself as illumined and all others as blind.

The empirical method which regards democracy as an hypothesis, warranted by its consequences for weal and woe, holds out some promise of reaching agreement provided human beings can be induced to follow its lead in social affairs as in physical affairs. If we ask, then, why we should treat individuals of unequal talents and endowments as persons who are equally entitled to relevant consideration and care—the central idea underlying democratic institutions—we can point to consequences of the following *type:* it makes for greater tranquillity, justice, freedom, security, creative diversity, reasonableness, and less cruelty, insensitiveness, and intellectual intolerance than any other social system that has so far been devised or proposed.[3] There are more widespread commitments among men to these values, and a greater agreement on the methods by which evidence is reached concerning whether or not they are present in any situation, than to any metaphysical or theological system which allegedly underlies them. Any one of these values has been or can be challenged in the course of experience. Its rejection or vindication depends on whether or not it furthers other values. There is no last resting point, nor is there a circle. We rest at each problem, until a new one arises.

This may be and has been contested by those who assert that there are ultimate values which are inarbitrable and that in the end only a radically ungrounded choice can be made when these ultimate values conflict. Existentialism is one of a variety of philosophical positions which stress the alleged fact of these ultimate values as a reason for denying or limiting the relevance of rational, scientific inquiry to problems of moral conflict.

Whether there are "ultimate" values for which we can offer no further justification or good reason is something which cannot be settled by fiat. It is a question of fact, not of definition. If there are such ultimate values, they may all be equally objective even if not universal. And if there are such ultimate

[3] For an amplification of this point, cf. my essay, "Naturalism and Democracy," in *Naturalism and the Human Spirit* (ed. Y. H. Krikorian; New York: Columbia University Press; 1944), pp. 40–64.

values, it is clear from the complex chains of justification which are offered in defense of myriads of policies and decisions, that they are very few in number. An overwhelming number of value conflicts would be still arbitrable in the light of some shared ultimate or terminal value.

Further, when we analyze judgments of value in the problematic contexts in which they are made, we invariably find in the structure of the situation a reference to what is the case or might very well be the case that has a bearing upon the validity of the judgment. Taken out of context, out of a real situation of danger and choice, the answer to the question: Should I live or not? may seem ultimate or arbitrary in the sense that no further justification can be given. Examined in the actual, living context in which a genuine problem arises whether one should live or die, a thousand good or bad reasons may suggest themselves for doing one or the other. Theoretically, it is *possible* that those who differ in their judgments of value in any specific situation may agree about all the facts involved and all the consequences for themselves and others likely to follow from the envisaged alternatives. If and when this is the case, we may speak of the difference in value judgment as ultimate. So far, I have never found a situation of strong value conflict in which this *is* the case. Conflicts over values seem always associated with conflicting assessments of causes and consequences. As far as the justification of democracy is concerned against its communist or fascist critics, I have always found that the argument seems to depend directly or indirectly upon judgments of fact. This would seem to indicate that the conflict of values is here not ultimate but penultimate.

(c) On the level of character and personality, the aim of education should be the development of intelligence. Here we reach the key value in the sense that it is both an end and the means of testing the validity of all other ends—moral, social, and educational. How is it to be justified? Why should we educate for intelligence? Once again, the answers divide into those which reply in terms of the antecedent nature of man, and those which point to the consequences of intelligence in use. These consequences are many and desirable. Intelligence enables us to break the blind routines of habit when confronted by new difficulties, to discover alternatives when uninformed impulse would thrust us into action, to foresee what cannot be avoided and to control what can. Intelligence helps us to discern the means by which to instate possibilities; to reckon costs before they are brought home; to order our community, our household, and our own moral economy. All this and more, in addition to the joys of understanding.

Whether man is intelligent, and how intelligent, and what conditions his intelligence, are empirical questions on which considerable evidence has accumulated. One might, of course, ask: What must the nature of man be in order for him to become intelligent? And if anyone can derive from the answer more illumination than he had before, we can reply: Man must potentially have the nature of a rational creature in order to *become* intelligent. How little this tells us is apparent when we reflect that it is tautological, except possibly for cases of mutation, to assert that a thing possesses potentially the qualities and relations it actually exhibits in the course of its development. Potentialities may not all be realized but, in a certain sense, everything realized may be regarded as potential prior to the moment of its actualization. Men are and may become unintelligent, too. Unintelligence (or stupidity) is therefore also an antecedent potentiality. But since, potentially, man is both intelligent *and* unintelligent, what we select as the trait to encourage depends not merely on its potentiality but rather on its desirability. And desirability is an affair of fruits, not of origins.

Growth, democracy, and intelligence are related, inclusive aims which obviously embrace all but two of the educational ends enumerated at the beginning of this chapter. The place of vocational education will be considered in a separate chapter. Here I should like to say a few words in justification of the trait of independence. In every society, not excluding democracy, there is a certain suspicion of the nonconformist and a fear of appearing different. "Man," Santayana somewhere writes, "is a gregarious animal and much more so in his mind than in his body. He may like to go alone for a walk but he hates to stand alone in his opinion." This is not less true for our modern socialized world in which powerful pressures are making for uniformity of taste and opinion. The intellectual heretic, the protagonist of the variant in arts and letters, the unintegrated and unpoliticalized talent, run greater risks today of being victimized by hostile sanctions, official and unofficial, than in the last century when our economy was more loose-jointed. To strengthen intellectual courage—that rarest of virtues—so that the individual may more readily withstand the tyranny of fashions is to increase the variety and goods in experience. Despite social hostility to the intellectual outsider, his work not infrequently redounds to the benefit of society. Even where it does not, independence gives the individual a certain distance from his own work and prevents him from becoming *merely* a public or political character. There must be some private altars in a public world where the human spirit can refresh itself. A liberal education should enable individuals, without failing in their social responsibilities, to build such altars and to nurse their flames.

What I have been doing is illustrating the mode of procedure which an experimentalist follows in justifying the ends of education. Different ends may be proposed but intelligent decision among them can be made only by canvassing their consequences in experience. These ends may, of course, be supported by theologians and metaphysicians, too. They may *add* reasons drawn from their private store of principles to justify supporting them. But from the point of view of the experimentalist, it is illegitimate to make these supplementary reasons necessary articles of faith without which the ends in question cannot be consistently or sincerely held. In the light of the history of thought, it is clear that agreement on certain social and moral ends is possible among men whose theological and metaphysical presuppositions are incompatible with each other. It is also clear that it is possible for men to share the same set of presuppositions, and yet to invoke them in support of ends and practices of an antithetical character. This suggests that our grounds for accepting or rejecting human values are actually independent logically of our grounds for accepting or rejecting their alleged presuppositions. It further suggests that the evidence drawn from the fruits and consequences of the way in which ideals function in experience is far more warranted than the evidence for theological or metaphysical assumptions. The possibility is therewith established of broadening the area of moral and social agreement among men and building a better world on human foundations long before agreement has been won on first or last things.

Chapter 3

THE NATURE OF MAN

"They say that habit is second nature. Who knows but that nature is first habit?"   PASCAL

WE HAVE been attempting to justify the ends of education by their consequences in experience. There is another approach which rules out all reference to consequences as irrelevant. This declares that we are dealing with a metaphysical question, which requires an answer based on the true metaphysics. Its chief exponents in America are Robert M. Hutchins, Monsignor Fulton Sheen, and Mortimer Adler. They hold that the appropriate end of education can be *deduced* from the true nature of man. The true nature of man is that which differentiates him from animals, on the one hand, and angels, on the other. It is expressed in the proposition: "Man is a rational animal." From which it is inferred that the end of human education should be the cultivation of reason.

We shall have occasion to see that the term "reason" does not mean the same thing as the term "intelligence"—that it designates something that has a different origin, nature, and function. But for present purposes, we shall ignore the differences in the meanings of the terms "reason" and "intelligence." The main point is that a patent fallacy is involved in the presumed deduction of the ends of education from what uniquely differentiates man from other animals.

First of all, if what we have previously said is true, from what man *is* we can at best reach conclusions only about what human education is, not what it *should be*. What man should be is undoubtedly related to what he is, for no man should be what he cannot be. Yet a proposition about what he is no more uniquely entails what he should be than the recognition of the nature of an egg necessitates our concluding that the egg should become a chicken rather than an egg sandwich.

A further assumption of the argument is the Aristotelian doctrine that the good of anything is the performance of its specific virtue or the realization of its potentiality. The "good" egg is one that becomes a chicken, the "good" man is one who realizes his natural capacity to think. This overlooks the fact that the natural capacities of a thing limit the range of its fulfillments but do not determine any specific fulfillment. Not every natural power of man has only one natural end; and not every power which has one end achieves it by one mode of development. Thinking is no more or no less natural to man than eating and singing. But what, when, and how a man should eat; what, when, and how a man should sing; about what and when he should think—all this depends not so much upon the natural powers of eating, singing, or thinking as upon an ideal of fitness, appropriateness, or goodness, that is *not* given with natural powers but brought to bear *upon* them in social, historical, and personal experience. When we assert that men *should* be rational, we are not talking biology or metaphysics but voicing a social directive that selectively modifies the natural exercise of human powers in the light of preferred consequences among possible alternate uses.

Second, granted for the sake of the argument that animals other than man are incapable of any rationality. The question is an old and difficult one, handled satirically by Plutarch and experimentally by Köhler, both of whom disagree with the airy dogmatism of the neo-Thomists. Nonetheless, rationality is not the only feature which differentiates man from other animals. Man can be defined, and has been by Benjamin Franklin and

Karl Marx, as a "tool-making animal." By the same reasoning employed by neo-Thomists, we can "deduce" that man's proper education should be vocational! Man is also the only animal that can will to commit suicide. Does it follow that education should therefore be a preparation for death? Man is also the only animal that ruts all year round. What educational corollary does this unique trait entail?

Thirdly, even if man is a rational animal, he is not only that. He has many other traits—needs, feelings, emotions, desires, whose nobility or ignobility depend upon their social context. An education appropriate to man would not necessarily limit itself to one aspect of his nature even if that aspect were regarded as more valuable than any other. It is a queer view of the nature of any organism that limits itself to a concern only with its differentia. The notion that the education of reason can or should be carried out independently of the education of the emotions has been called by Whitehead "one of the most fatal, erroneous and dangerous conceptions ever introduced into the theory of education."[1] At any rate what is clear is that we can go from the nature of man to the conclusion that we should educate for reason only because some selective principle has been introduced. The basic educational issues, like the basic ethical issues, pose problems of choice. The nature of man is always relevant; but just as relevant is our decision as to what we want to make of it, what we want men to become. At this point no metaphysical deduction, whether proceeding from materialistic or spiritualistic premises concerning the nature of "reality," can guide us.

What, after all, is meant by "*the* nature of man" whenever we speak of relating educational ends to it? The phrase masks a certain ambiguity that makes it difficult to tell whether its reference is empirical or metaphysical. A great deal of philosophical profundity consists in shifting back and forth between these two references and not being found out. When the neo-

[1] Alfred North Whitehead: *The Aims of Education and Other Essays* (New York: The Macmillan Company; 1929), p. 9.

Thomists speak of *the* nature of man as a basis for educational ideals, their concern is not primarily with biological, psychological, historical, and social features of human behavior. For since these items designate specific processes of *interaction* between an organism and its environment, it would be risky to choose any set of traits as fixing forever *the* nature of human nature, and therefore *the* nature of education. But the position we are examining is concerned precisely with a conception of human nature which will permit the deduction that, in the words of Mr. Hutchins, "education should everywhere be the same." Everywhere and at every time? Everywhere and at every time. In a weakened form, Mr. Adler repeats this: "If man is a rational animal, constant in nature through history, there must be certain constant features in every sound educational program regardless of culture and epoch."[2] And Mr. Mark van Doren, who carries all of his teacher's ideas to recognizable absurdity, adds that because education and democracy have the same end—the making of men—they are one and the same. "So education is democracy and democracy is education."[3] From man's nature we can apparently deduce not only that education should everywhere be the same, but the social system, too.

If education is determined by human nature, may not human nature change, and with it the nature of education? *"We must insist,"* writes Mr. Hutchins, *"that no matter how environments differ human nature is, always has been, and always will be the same everywhere."*[4]

This is truly a remarkable assertion. Before we inquire on what evidence Mr. Hutchins knows this to be true, let us see what it implies. For one thing, it implies that human nature is

[2] Mortimer Adler: "The Crisis in Contemporary Education," *Social Frontier,* Vol. 5, No. 42 (February 1939), p. 140.
[3] Mark van Doren: *Liberal Education* (New York: Henry Holt & Company; 1943), p. 38.
[4] Robert M. Hutchins. "Towards a Durable Society," *Fortune,* Vol. 27, No. 6 (June 1943), p. 158. My italics.

completely independent of changes in the world of physical nature with which the human organism is in constant interaction. Now, certainly, Mr. Hutchins cannot know that the world of nature "is, always has been, and always will be the same everywhere." He therefore must believe that no transformation of the physical basis of human life can possibly affect human nature. His assertion further implies that man's nature is completely independent of changes in the human body, particularly the brain and nervous system. At one stroke this calls into question the whole evolutionary approach to the origin and development of the human species. Finally, it implies that the habitation of man's nature in a human body is unaffected by changes in society and social nurture. The enormous range of variation in social behavior, which testifies to the plasticity of the simplest physiological response under cultural conditioning, leaves the essence of human nature unaltered. In short, human nature is taken out of the world altogether. It is removed from any verifiable context in experience which would permit us to identify it and observe its operations. For anything which operates in the world does so in *interaction* with other things that help shape its character.

There is only one entity that satisfies all these conditions. It is the supernatural soul as conceived by theologians of the orthodox Christian tradition. It is not the Aristotelian concept of the soul because, for Aristotle, the soul was the form of the body, all forms were incarnate in matter, and the nature of man was construed from his behavior. The constancy of human nature in Aristotle was predicated on the notion of the constancy of the natural order as well. Were he, in the light of modern science, to abandon the latter notion, he would have surrendered the belief in the constancy of human nature, since it was integrally related to the behavior of the body in nature and society. For Aristotle man can become a rational animal only because he is also a social and physical animal. But Mr. Hutchins admits all the facts of physical and biological change as well as historical and social development in man's *environment*, yet insists that man's nature cannot change or develop. It is only when we realize that he is not talking about empirical, historical, suffering man but about a mystical, supernatural entity, which has a temporary abode in the human body, that the peculiarities and ambiguities of his language are understandable.

This is the secret behind the talk of man's true and constant nature that defies all change. Bishop Sheen and M. Maritain are more frank with us than their epigoni at Chicago and elsewhere. But all of them owe us a proof that the immortal soul, as defined by them, exists. So far not a shred of valid experimental evidence has been adduced to warrant belief in its existence. In fact, the achievements of genuine knowledge about human nature in medicine, biology, psychology, and history have been largely won by a bitter struggle against obstacles set in the path of scientific inquiry by believers in a supernatural soul.

When it is understood that by "human nature" Hutchins really means the human soul, whose study involves rational theology, and whose goal cannot be adequately grasped without the deliverances of sacred theology and revealed religion, another article of his educational faith becomes clear. The true education of man must include the education of his soul by the one true metaphysics and theology. In the writings of Mr. Hutchins this conclusion is obliquely expressed, but it is explicitly drawn in those of his mentor, Mr. Adler. "Sacred theology is superior to philosophy, both theoretically and practically. . . . Just as there are no systems of philosophy but only philosophical knowledge less or more adequately possessed by different men, so there is only one true religion, less or more adequately embodied in the existing diversity of creeds."[5] To

[5] Mortimer Adler: "God and the Professors," in *Proceedings of the Conference on Science, Philosophy and Religion* (ed. Louis Finkelstein; New York: Harper & Brothers; 1940), p. 131.

this he adds the claim that anyone who does not accept the truth of these propositions has no logical right to call himself, or be regarded, as a democrat, together with the urgent recommendation that all teachers who do not subscribe to these truths should be purged ("liquidated" is his word) from our culture.

Since the central problem of education is for Mr. Hutchins a metaphysical problem, all the basic issues depend for their solution upon finding *the* true metaphysical answer. Consequently, metaphysics, including rational theology, occupies the chief place in the recommended curriculum of studies as the only discipline that can impart to students a rational view of the world. "By way of metaphysics," he writes, "students on their part may recover a rational view of the universe and of their role in it. If you deny this proposition you take the responsibility of asserting that a rational view of the universe and one's place in it is no better than an irrational one or none at all."[6]

The philosophic presumption of this passage vies with its atrocious logic. To deny the proposition "by way of metaphysics students may recover a rational view of the universe" is certainly *not* to assert that "a rational view of the universe . . . is no better than an irrational one or none at all." The denial of the first proposition implies that students cannot get a rational view of the universe by way of metaphysics; it leaves open the possibility that they may get a rational view of the universe by the study of *other* disciplines, e.g. the sciences, social studies, literature, and history. It emphatically does not imply that a rational conception of the universe is worthless or worth no more than an irrational one. I pass over the additional confusion of identifying a rational conception of the world with the conception that men are rational and the world rationally ordered. A rational conception is one warranted by evidence and a conception of the world may be rational *if* the

[6] Robert M. Hutchins: *Education for Freedom* (Baton Rouge: Louisiana State University Press; 1943), pp. 26–7.

evidence points to the fact that men are irrational and the world chaotic. I am not saying they are, but contesting the relevance of an a priori metaphysical deduction to these questions. Nor am I denying that the study of philosophy has an important place in the liberal arts curriculum. It has many justifications—among them the achievement of a methodological sophistication that may immunize students against the confusion of definitions or linguistic resolutions with empirical hypotheses of varying degrees of generality, which constitutes so much of traditional and popular metaphysics.

It is important to know what men are in order intelligently to determine what they should become. Educational aims merely restate what we believe men should become insofar as they can be influenced by the processes of learning and teaching. The comparative study of cultures shows how diverse men may become; it also shows certain similarities and identities. The vital physiological sequences are the same in every culture. A social organization, a form of mating, and other institutions are also everywhere observable where men live together. But there are all types and degrees of cultural institutions. And these institutions, in turn, give varied meanings to identical physiological acts. These meanings enter so integrally into the performance of the physiological action that it requires an abstract science like biology to distinguish between what is attributable to the unlearned behavior of the organism and what is learned from the culture. "It would be idle," says Malinowski, "to disregard the fact that the impulse leading to the simplest physiological performance is as highly plastic and determined by tradition as it is ineluctable in the long run because determined by physiological necessities."[7] Depending upon the particular aspect of human behavior we are interested

[7] Bronislaw Malinowski: *A Scientific Theory of Culture and Other Essays* (ed. Huntington Cairns; Chapel Hill: University of North Carolina Press; 1944), p. 87.

in, we can establish an empirical case for the constancy or mutability of human nature. Provided we keep the distinctions in mind, there is nothing incompatible in asserting that in certain respects human nature is the same, in others different. What is apparent is that those aspects of human nature which appear constant are a set of unconscious processes that are a condition of life. Although these are taken note of in every sensible educational program, they are far from the center of educational concern, which is understanding the dominant cultural problems of the present in relation to the past out of which they have grown, and to the future whose shape depends in part upon that understanding. Whether men remain the same or different, in the sense in which the question is educationally significant, depends upon whether they choose to retain or transform their culture.

The whole question of the constancy of human nature is sometimes obscured by a simple failure to distinguish between names and things. The name we give anything originally fixes our attention on it and identifies it as the object whose behavior (or nature) we are going to inquire into. After we have discovered its behavior, the name is used not only to identify the thing but as a shorthand indication of selected traits of its behavior. If and when these traits change, it becomes a matter of convention whether we are going to continue using the same name or some other name to designate the new properties. If we decide to use another name, this by no means gainsays the historical fact that the traits which hitherto have constituted the nature of the thing have changed or been modified. This is denied in the following passage which is typical of members of the school we are discussing: "The most familiar form of the problem [permanence and change] has to do with the nature of man, concerning which the educated person will know what he knows about any nature, namely that insofar as it is a nature, it does not change. For then we should have another nature; meaning that in the case of man he would have another name."[8]

Apparently an educated man cannot distinguish between things and names. Names are intelligently used to communicate knowledge and facilitate the control of things. The names we choose to attach to things have no bearing on how they actually are going to behave; they summarize what our experience has led us to believe they will do. The argument of the passage is equivalent to saying that what comes from a cow's udders can never become material for apparel because, since the first we call "milk" and the second "cloth," their essential natures must be different. Milk *cannot* change into cloth. How can a metaphysical bull, in its triple sense, determine that what comes from a cow's udders must be drunk by human beings, instead, after appropriate treatment, of being turned into cloth for apparel? The whole of modern science would come to a stop if it took this word-magic seriously. Since the changes that men undergo are part of their nature, it is absurd to argue from a definition of the *term* "human nature" that human nature throughout its long historical pilgrimage has not changed and cannot change. For if this be true by definition, it is an analytic statement or tautology that does not tell us anything about the world (except about how a certain writer proposes to use a certain word). But those who write this way set great store by statements of this kind as momentous truths about men.

In conclusion. To speak of *the* nature of man is already a sign that a selective interest is present. What is designated by the term "man" may have many natures depending upon the context and purpose of inquiry. Even if *the* nature of man is defined in terms of what differentiates him from other animals, we can choose any one of a number of diverse traits that will satisfy the formal conditions of the definition. And for many purposes what man has in common with other animals may

[8] Van Doren: *Liberal Education*, p. 26.

not be irrelevant to his nature. Once we assign a term to stand for a thing and seek to discover its nature, that nature is disclosed not by a definition and its logical implications, as in mathematics, but in its activity or behavior. The activity or behavior of man depends upon many things within and outside of his body. From the point of view of education, the most important of the forces beyond the skin of a man's body which control his behavior is the culture of which he is a part. It also controls many things that occur beneath his skin. Human history is an eloquent record of cultural change, of continuities and discontinuities, in social institutions, language, values, and ideas. It is therefore the sheerest dogmatism to deny that human nature can change.

Education should be adequate to man. Man's nature does not change. Therefore an education adequate to man will always be the same. So Mr. Hutchins and his fellow-metaphysicians argue.

Education should be adequate to man. Man's nature shows a pattern of development in which both constant and variable elements may be discerned. Therefore an education adequate to man will reveal a pattern that reflects this development. So the experimentalist educator.

Value judgments underlie both positions. But the first can be held only so long as the term "human nature" is an unanalyzable abstraction. Just as soon as an empirical meaning is given it, its falsity is palpable. The fact that certain specific educational proposals—like an identical curriculum for all students—are justified by the alleged universal constancy of "human nature" indicates that the term is being used with systematic ambiguity.

The task of the experimentalist is by no means exhausted in exposing the errors and illogic of metaphysical dogmatism in education. He must go on to discover what an education adequate for modern man is, and to test the validity of all practical proposals in respect to content and method—no matter what their source—which promise to achieve it. His hope is to develop an educational program for modern man whose fruits in experience will be so rich that it may be accepted by all democrats independently of their metaphysical prepossessions.

Chapter 4

SOCIETY AND EDUCATION

"The fading of ideals is sad evidence of the defeat of human endeavor."
A. N. WHITEHEAD

THAT EVERY educational system intimately reflects the society in which it functions is a commonplace truth. Like all commonplaces it acquires relevance when ignored and importance when denied. It is ignored whenever a scheme of education is proposed for *immediate* adoption that would require the complete transformation of the social order. True educational wisdom must be more than a counsel of perfection; its suggested reforms should use what is good in an inadequate situation to make the whole better. Otherwise it provides no leverage for action and runs out into denunciation or fantasy. The actual is rarely desirable, but what is educationally desirable must at least be possible within the historical actuality in which the educator finds himself.

We find this commonplace denied whenever an educational pattern which has proved satisfactory for one society is taken as a standard of excellence for another society, without regard to the needs and problems characteristic of the latter. We may *define* a good education as one that plays a certain integrative role within its culture and in this sense a good education will *formally* be the same in every culture. But from this it does not follow in the least that any *course of study* will be "the same at any time, in any place, under any political, social or economic conditions."[1]

As in the discussion of educational ends, two types of related questions must be distinguished if customary confusions about the role of education in society are to be avoided. One is the historical question as to the actual role education *has* played in different societies, past and present. The second is the normative question as to what role education *should* play. If a concrete proposal is made that education play a role which historical evidence reveals as defying all reasonable likelihood, reasonable people will abandon it. In this way, the facts exercise a veto, not a legislative, power. But within the limits which they make possible, the historical facts alone do not determine what education's role should be. Certain areas for large choices are left open and the responsibility for one variant or another is ours, not history's.

In its broadest and least controversial sense, education may be defined as the assimilation of the culture of any society, and its transmission from one generation to another. "Culture" is here used in its anthropological meaning, current since Tylor, as denoting a complex of institutions, tools, techniques, traditions, and values. In this sense, it is clear that no society can perpetuate itself without education. It is also obvious that many societies exist in which education proceeds *without formal schooling*. In primitive societies education goes on without schools. As is the case within some fields of existing society, education takes place within life situations, not classrooms. Today, even our youngest children have received some education before they are sent to school. Otherwise they could hardly benefit from schooling.

[1] Robert M. Hutchins: *The Higher Learning in America* (New Haven: Yale University Press; 1936), p. 66.

Formal schooling develops comparatively late in the history of culture, and for a variety of causes. The rise of institutional religion and the necessity of training for the priesthood; problems of government arising from internal growth or external conquest which require the preparation of rulers and administrators, military and civil; division of labor which calls for the mastery of special techniques or for a basic literacy as a pre-condition, especially in machine cultures, of vocational skills; social rifts and conflicts that imperil traditional values and conventions which formal schooling is expected to reinforce—these are some of the causes of the emergence of schools as explicit agencies of instruction.

All school education in every society performs one or the other, and usually both, of two functions. The first is the imparting of certain techniques, skills, and bodies of knowledge. The second is the inculcation, with more or less deliberateness, of generic attitudes and habits of evaluation to a point where they become a part of the unreflective behavior pattern of those who have undergone the educational process. On some levels of educational activity in some corners of modern society, the attitudes and habits of evaluation thus inculcated are brought into the light of reflective consciousness. But this is a very unusual phenomenon.

Of the two phases of the educational process, the latter is logically prior—whatever the historical order may have been—because the kind of techniques, skills, and bodies of knowledge selected for instruction, as well as the desirability of such instruction, depend upon what those who control the educational activity in any society regard as being of most worth.

In all societies, whether the fact be deplored or approved, the prevailing education serves a social purpose. It is not autonomous; is does not set up its own goals. But although the school always serves a social purpose, it must not be assumed that this purpose is a constant one in all societies. The *kind* of social purpose which the school exercises varies with the kind of society in which it is found, and with different stages of social development—a consideration which is of crucial importance when we analyze the purposes of the school in a *democratic* society.

That the educational activities within a society reflect in divers ways the character of the society and its dominant ideals has been recognized by thinkers, great and small, from the days of Plato and Aristotle to the present. In Plato, whose solutions are total, this led to a demand, not only in the *Republic* but also in the *Laws*, that the whole of society be revolutionized as a condition for instituting the best education. Aristotle, like Plato, makes the good state dependent upon a good education but, recognizing that different states might be good in different ways in different historical circumstances, he is more interested in improving the education he finds than in building it over from top to bottom. He emphasizes the role education in fact plays in all communities, and complains that not sufficient regard is given to this role, so that the possibilities of exploiting it for the interest of a better education in any given society are neglected. "But of all things which I have mentioned that which most contributes to the permanence of constitutions is the adaptation of education to the form of government, and yet in our own day this is universally neglected. The best laws, though sanctioned by every citizen of the state, will be of no avail, unless the young are trained by habit and education in the spirit of the constitution, if the laws are democratic, democratically, oligarchically, if the laws are oligarchical."[2]

Napoleon, despite his scorn of the *ideologues*, agreed with them in recognizing the place of education in the social order. "Of all political questions that [of education] is perhaps the most important art. There cannot be a firmly established po-

[2] Aristotle: *Politics* (tr. Benjamin Jowett; New York: Random House; 1943), 1310a 12–17.

litical state unless there is a teaching body with definitely recognized principles."[3]

The theoretical spokesmen of Italian Fascism, Giovanni Gentile, expressed the same idea in murky, neo-Hegelian language. "The State's active and dynamic consciousness is a system of thought, of ideas, of interests to be satisfied and of morality to be realized. Hence, the state is, as it ought to be, a teacher; it maintains and develops schools to promote this morality. In the school, the State comes to a consciousness of its real being."[4]

Lenin, the founder of the Russian Soviet State, declared with brutal frankness and characteristic oversimplification what so many others have hinted at by gentle indirection. "The more cultured the bourgeois state, the more subtly did it lie when it declared that the school could stand above politics and serve society as a whole. As a matter of fact, the school was turned into nothing but an instrument of the class rule of the bourgeoisie. Its purpose was to supply the capitalists with obedient lackeys and intelligent workers. . . . We publicly declare that education divorced from life and politics is a lie and hypocrisy."[5]

In these sentiments Stalin and Khrushchev have been faithful disciples, as the startling changes in the Russian educational system eloquently show. The explanation of why Russian children of one generation were taught to revere "Ivan the Good," while their fathers were taught to execrate "Ivan the Terrible," is to be found neither in the advance of scholarship nor in the tortured justifications of apologists about a new historical synthesis, but in the plain political fact that Russian revolutionary internationalism had been replaced by no less dangerous

[3] Quoted by I. Kandel in article "Education," *Encyclopedia of the Social Sciences*, Vol. 5 (New York: The Macmillan Company; 1942), p. 415.
[4] Quoted by H. W. Schneider and S. B. Clough in *Making Fascists* (Chicago: University of Chicago Press; 1929), p. 85.
[5] N. Lenin: *Collected Works* (English translation; New York: International Publishers Co., Inc.; 1945), Vol. 23, p. 215.

Russian imperialistic nationalism. This, and this alone, made sense of the slogan: "Every boy a soldier and every girl a mother." After the Second World War, when the consequences of the breakthrough in the field of nuclear energy became clear, the whole of Soviet education was reoriented to produce under forced draft the technological specialists who would give the Soviet Union a commanding lead in the race for world victory.

What of the role of education in America? That it reflects the American political, social, and economic scene in many ways is too obvious to need elaboration. But I cannot resist quoting a *defense* of American education against retrenchment which expresses with a kind of blissful aplomb one of the functions assigned by large taxpayers to the schools. "Those who seek to escape or to reduce nationally the taxes on their property and incomes today by demanding the impoverishment of the current educational program would do well to consider what may be the future of their possessions if we should be so foolish as to permit this sacrifice, and *thereby promote the future decay of the very institution which most effectively assures the private ownership and enjoyment of property and incomes.*"[6]

The history of the last twenty years would indicate that the schools have perhaps failed in performing the function assigned to them. But it opens up the questions: What functions have the schools in fact served in American democracy? Is it true that the schools have exercised precisely the *same* social roles in American political democracy as in Fascist Italy or Bolshevik Russia? What functions *can* the schools serve? What functions *should* they serve?

Before approaching these problems, I wish to consider a possible inference that an unwary reader might draw from this survey of the relation between schools and society. Since educa-

[6] From the text of a radio address by Professor Harley Lutz of Princeton University over NBC, April 29, 1933. My italics.

cation reflects, or is a product of, society, it might appear that the *only* way in which education can be transformed is by the transformation of society. This is the view of Mr. Hutchins, who began by proposing a scheme to revolutionize first education and then society, and has now concluded that, since education can rise no higher than its social source, it is society that must first be revolutionized. The goodness or badness of education is both a sign and an effect of the goodness or badness of the society.

"The question most often put to me is: 'What is wrong with our educational system?' The answer to this question is: 'Nothing. . . .'

"The answer to the question asked me may, however, be given in somewhat more general terms. There is never anything wrong with the educational system of a country. What is wrong is the country. The educational system that any country has will be the system that country wants."[7]

The moral is that there is no hope of changing the character of education to any significant degree unless the country is changed. And so the circle completes itself from educational utopianism, 'society can be changed only by changing its system of education,' to educational defeatism, 'no change in education is possible without changing society.' Interestingly enough, this type of defeatism—expressed in the proposition that educational change is futile without social change—coincides with the view of that variety of orthodox, doctrinaire Marxism which insists that education everywhere is in every essential always tied to the exigencies of political power, and consequently educational reformers are willy-nilly lieutenants of the capitalist class on the educational front.[8] The difference between the Hutchins school and this variety of orthodox

[7] Robert M. Hutchins: *Education for Freedom* (Baton Rouge: Louisiana State University Press; 1943), p. 48.
[8] A typical expression of doctrinaire Marxism of this brainless variety will be found in H. D. Langford: *Education and the Social Conflict* (New York: The Macmillan Company; 1936).

Marxism is that the first advocates the transformation of society by a spiritual revolution led by men of superior theological and metaphysical insight, whereas the second looks to revolution in the mode of economic production led by professional revolutionists in the name of the proletariat. Both suffer from simplistic, monistic conceptions of social causation.

That educational changes by themselves are sufficient to effect basic social changes, and that a profound educational transformation can get under way without profound social changes, are, both of them, mistaken views. But that education can accomplish little or nothing in changing society, and that widespread reforms in education are impossible until the country lifts itself by its bootstraps, are views that are just as mistaken. The opposite of an absurdity, F. H. Bradley once remarked, may be every whit as absurd. Although the above disjunctions in the possibilities of action may exclude each other, they certainly do not exhaust all the alternatives.

The question of what education can or cannot do is not to be settled by definition, nor by an induction from one or two selected but unanalyzed cases. When we look closely at all the instances cited, we find that although it is true that education always serves society in *some* way, it is not true that it everywhere serves society in the *same* way. More specifically, the way education serves society in a political democracy is different from the way it serves society when political democracy is dead or not yet born.

Even in a politically undemocratic society education can achieve, and has achieved, significant things. It has bolstered up a decaying social order by strengthening allegiance to undefined symbols that are skillfully associated with scepter and crown or church institutions. It has knit together the most diverse elements of a population in crusades and wars. It has profoundly influenced fashion ranging all the way from ideas to tastes in food. It has sometimes aided in the creation of great art and science.

But in an undemocratic society there is one thing education has never done and cannot do. It cannot influence the reformation of social policy or the redirection of social change. For the control of educational facilities is a monopoly of the politically dominant minority. It usually emanates from a single and central agency. The content of instruction is under careful supervision. The whole process of education is carried on with an ideological self-consciousness to a degree hardly suspected by those who have not studied the mechanisms of control. In such a society, education certainly has a social function; but it rarely serves the interests of the community as a whole or of a majority within the community. Ideas that contribute to weakening the hold of the dominant group in society, as in pre-revolutionary France, are ideas that are ignored or combatted in the official schools. This remains true even if we recognize that on the eve of profound social changes, when the community is wracked by open conflict, the struggle expresses itself also in the educational agencies of the old order.

In a politically democratic society, education can do much more, for good or evil, in influencing social policy than in nondemocratic societies. It is the failure to note this which accounts for the confrontation in much educational discussion of the simple alternatives of utopianism and defeatism. In a democratic society, education is not a *monopoly* of one group. Nor is it as centralized as in other societies. A variety of conflicting influences play upon the content and goals of teaching even though some of these influences, emanating from groups close to the sources of economic power, carry a much greater weight than others. The actual profession of the formal ideals of democracy—government by consent, freedom of opposition, freedom of speech, press, and inquiry—may have practical consequences even when such profession is confused. It enables new ideas to get a fairer hearing than in other social systems. More important, it permits critical attitudes of thought to develop. And, more important still, these ideas and attitudes in a democratic society pervade other areas of social life. It would be difficult to explain the history of American social legislation without reference to the influence, mediated by mass education, which the ideal of "equality of opportunity" —so far from being carried out even in our educational system!—has had in formulating pointed demands for *more* democracy in other fields. Whoever seeks to explain the complicated, overlapping, richly confused patterns of American education in terms of the political or economic interests of a "power elite" either misconceives the nature of political power or of an elite or both. For in the medley of forces affecting American education, the influence of Main Street is and has been far more decisive than that of Wall Street.

Democrats are painfully aware of the depressing record of restrictions upon freedom of inquiry, freedom of teaching and learning, in the educational affairs of a democracy. The point is, however, that they *are* aware of them as lapses in a democracy; that they do not take them as natural or as a matter of course, which is the case in other forms of society; and that they do not have to appeal to an alien ideology to find a standard by which to judge them. The moral difficulty, the shadow of educational insincerity and social hypocrisy, falls on those who fail to live up to the profession of democratic ideals, not on those who press for their realization. It is true that formal allegiance to democratic ideals in education is often no more than a holiday proclamation. But it is also true that just as often they are realized in the workaday activities of the school. And with a little courage they could be more often realized. These ideals are too readily dismissed as "rationalizations" because of their imperfect embodiment. But even as "rationalizations" they count to the extent that the language of reason makes some difference.

The influence of continued invocation of the ideals of equal opportunity, of commitment to the defense of human rights, first against Hitler and subsequently against Stalin and

Khrushchev, has made itself felt in the slow, unfortunately-too-gradual, but sure erosion of the practice of racial segregation in many areas of American life. Those who still oppose integration are fighting a losing battle because, among other reasons, they are fighting against their own best sense of fairness, dignity, and human equality, the very ideals to which they appeal when they feel themselves the victims of aggression.

In a political democracy, to be sure, education is controlled. But the controls are various. They are not all in the hands of one group. And the groups that control do so with varying degrees of consciousness. The very lack of doctrinal cohesion in a democracy, which so many democrats shortsightedly deplore, makes it possible for educators to project ideas and practices which need not be *identical* with the forms and practices of democracy as they exist at any given time. It is only in a democracy that the state need not fear the competition of other educational agencies, including private schools that are subsidized and controlled by special groups. This was brought home by an important event in the history of American education.

A generation ago, the people of the state of Oregon, after extensive public discussion, adopted by a popular referendum vote a law requiring children of certain ages to attend public schools. The constitutionality of the law was contested and the United States Supreme Court declared it invalid. Whatever one thinks of the wisdom of the law—and a strong case can be made out against it—the decision of the Court was notable for two things. The first was a striking confusion between the right of children to receive education *in addition* to that provided by public schools—which the statute did not abridge in the slightest—and their right to receive education in private schools from partisan agencies *as a substitute* for public education—which the statute aimed to prevent. Only the former is essential to democratic educational policy; the latter, under certain circumstances, may be an overt threat to democracy. The Court nullified the law on the ground that it forced children to accept instruction from "public teachers only." But this the law did not do. It permitted private schools and parents to give supplementary, even contrary, instruction to children of school age—after the relatively short hours of public schooling.

Nonetheless, more important than this confusion of the Court were the principles and language of its decision. They express so magnificently the recognition that the state has no monopoly of education in a democracy, that I cannot forbear quoting the central passage.

"The fundamental theory of liberty upon which all governments in the Union repose excludes any general power of the State to standardize its children by forcing them to accept instruction from public teachers only. The child is not the mere creature of the state; those who nurture him and direct his destiny have the right, coupled with the high duty, to recognize and prepare him for additional obligations."[9]

That the state has no monopoly of education is a principle which no totalitarian state can accept. The recognition, however, that there are plural sources and forms of education in a democracy must not be construed too naively. It does not bar the democratic state from taking measures to safeguard the integrity of the public sector of education against efforts on the part of private groups, religious or secular, to inject their dogmas into the content of education.

It would be easy to misunderstand what I am saying if it were interpreted as asserting that education in a political democracy can ever lead by itself to a fundamental transformation. The

[9] *Pierce v. Society of Sisters:* 268 U.S. 535 (1924). The opinion was written by Mr. Justice McReynolds.

schools *cannot* rebuild society. The decisive steps in social transformation depend upon crises that are prepared not by education but by the development of the underlying economy, existing technology, and the chances of war. What education can do is to prepare, through proper critical methods, the attitudes and ideals that come *focally* into play when crises arise. It can develop the long-term patterns of sensibility and judgment which *may* be decisive in resolving the short-term problems whose succession constitutes so much of the substance of contemporary history.

Education, then, has *some* influence on the social order in all societies, but much *more* influence in a democratic society than in any other. How much more is a function of specific historical situations, and of the intelligence and courage of educators. The practical corollary of this analysis is clear under the limiting conditions of all social action. *In a democracy, educators as a group have a greater opportunity to influence society, and therefore a greater responsibility for what they do or fail to do, than in any other political order.* Like all educators, the democratic educator serves society. But to serve society does not mean to be a servant of society or of the most influential classes within it. An educator who accepts the philosophy of democracy owes allegiance not to one group in the community or even primarily to the community as it is composed at any particular moment, but to a set of ideals and to a *method* which he believes commensurate to the task of validating these ideals.

We are now in a position to bring to light the stupendous and dangerous ambiguity expressed in the view of Mr. Alexander Meiklejohn, that *"the purpose of all teaching is to express the cultural authority of the group by which the teaching is given."*[1] The group by which the teaching is given does not mean for him the teachers: he means by it the society in

[1] Alexander Meiklejohn: *Education Between Two Worlds* (New York: Harper & Brothers; 1942), p. 91. Italics in text.

whose name they are hired by some governmental agency. Test this proposition by concrete reference to the *actual* teaching which goes on in a democratic community. *Where* or *in whom* does the "cultural authority" repose? Is it one group or many groups? The most obvious fact about a democratic community is the plurality of groups of which it is composed, and these are not always in agreement. What, then, is the character of the "cultural authority"? Is it the values which *all* groups in the community hold in common, or is it the values of the dominant group? *How* do teachers "express" the cultural authority of the group? By transmitting it as antecedent truth that cannot be rejected, or by critically appraising this authority as one proposal among others? Are the teachers hired by a community to teach the truth as they see it or as the community sees it? All of these questions can be clearly answered when we examine the actual role of teaching in totalitarian societies, for no one is in doubt as to who is master there. None of them can be clearly answered independently of the specific educational situation, when we turn to societies which we recognize as democratic. The answers will be different in Winnetka and Boston, Dayton and New York. "The purpose of education" in Mr. Meiklejohn's proposition slurs over essential differences in the role teachers can play and have played in different communities.

When Mr. Meiklejohn goes on to assert the proposition not merely as a description of what we might actually observe but as a judgment of what teaching *should* be, its moral inadequacy becomes palpable. It is just because teaching in a totalitarian community transmits the authority of the group that we condemn it. Nor do we hesitate to condemn the teaching in a politically democratic community whose cultural authority decrees that the content of instruction be fixed —whether in astronomy, biology, or social thought—irrespective of the weight of scientific evidence. A teacher is not disloyal who teaches the theory of evolution in a fundamentalist community.

Like so many ideas drawn from the ambiguous legacy of Rousseau, the doctrine that education *should* always transmit the cultural authority of the group unwittingly plays into the hands of totalitarians. This is such a serious charge that it requires further substantiation. If the purpose of teaching is to express the cultural authority of the group, and if the authority of the group is vested in the state, then the state, according to Mr. Meiklejohn, does and should determine the goal, methods, and content of teaching. "Education is an expression of the will of some social 'organism, instinct with one life, moved by one mind.' Teacher and pupil . . . are both agents of the state."[2] Does this not seem to imperil individual freedom? Even individuals as sympathetic to Mr. Meiklejohn as M. Maritain have confessed to a deep disquietude over these sentiments.[3]

Our fears are groundless, Mr. Meiklejohn assures us, because human freedom "is freedom in and by the state." The state is not an instrument which administers common interests and mediates between conflicting interests that arise from social life. Nor is it ever an agency of class rule. It is that without which men are not men. All we have, all we are, belongs to the state. It gives us our freedoms, it can rightfully set limits to them and take them away. It can compel us to be free for our own good. No one has any rights against the state. If it constrains us or punishes us, we are still free, for after all "a state is its members, ruling themselves, obeying themselves, in accordance with a general mind, a general will, which is their mind, their will." Certain irritating situations may crop up

[2] Ibid., p. 279.
[3] Jacques Maritain: *Education at the Crossroads* (New Haven: Yale University Press; 1943), p. 101. Cf. also Ernest Nagel on Meiklejohn's views in *The Humanist*, Vol. 3, new series, No. 2 (Summer 1943), p. 81.

in which there appears to be a conflict between ourselves and the state power, but this is an illusion produced by a false consciousness of self-interest. It vanishes when we grasp the underlying and unconscious reason and harmony of the state. "The state is the whole body of the people, consciously or unconsciously taking directions over its own activities and those of its members." Conflict with the state is a form of self-conflict and is resolved when we understand that "the state is the best of us, trying to control and elevate the worst of us."

With a post-nescience that is truly uncanny, Mr. Meiklejohn attributes these notions, whose source is Rousseau and Hegel, to Jefferson and the Founding Fathers. (He claims that Rousseau's thought influenced revolutionary America, a grave lapse in scholarship.) Yet on his own theory of the "unconscious direction" of the state by the people, it is difficult to explain how there ever could have been an American Revolution at all. Either Mr. Meiklejohn must believe that there was no English state at the time, or that the Revolution was an illusion of interested consciousness. He does not believe the latter. But if he believes there was no English state at the time of the American Revolution, then it is hard to see how he can believe that there ever was such a thing as a state as he defines it—or how there could be. His "state" is the social analogue of Mr. Hutchins' "reason": it is outside the world of time and history. Mr. Meiklejohn's language makes sense only on the assumption that he is discussing a community not of men on earth but of angels—who require neither state nor government. His language is dangerous because he does not distinguish between society, government, and state, or between existing states on earth and the perfect state in heaven. It is practically made to order for any cultural group which demands of its members complete conformity to its dictates on the ground that its will is their will "consciously or unconsciously." In a world where the state is growing stronger every day without overmuch concern for the rights of persons, it is an exaltation of the state in the name of freedom and reason.

Mr. Meiklejohn is acutely aware that his doctrine is open to the charge of giving ideological aid and comfort to totalitarianism. As a freedom-loving educator he is concerned to meet it in advance. He tells us that he agrees with only one of the two basic contentions of totalitarianism, that "the state must be strong and powerful, eager and able to achieve its purposes against all opposition within and without."[4] And one of its chief purposes, it should be borne in mind, is to see to it that education transmits its authority. The second contention, with which he disagrees, is that "the state can be strong and powerful only if it becomes a dictatorship. . . ." The trouble is that if one unconditionally accepts the first statement, one must on occasion swallow the consequences of the second, for the latter is sometimes in fact true. If Mr. Meiklejohn insists that a state *must* be strong and powerful, then whenever it is in fact true that this can be achieved only by a dictatorship, he is committed to it. One could argue, on the theory of the General Will, that in such a case the dictatorship is the rule of all the people, including its victims, and therefore a democracy in a higher sense. But that would be a rhetorical indecency. If we translate what we say about a strong and powerful state into observable effects, we discover that this always means making some human beings stronger and more powerful than others. For certain purposes this may be necessary to carry out collective decisions. But it is courting disaster to suppose that there will be no danger that they will be "eager and able" to achieve *their* purposes against *all* opposition within and without. May not the opposition be right? Or are the guardians of Mr. Meiklejohn's state, like those of Plato's, guaranteed to be creatures of golden virtue?

Mr. Meiklejohn sums up his rejoinder to the charge that he is unduly exalting the state over the freedom and dignity of the individual in a single assertion. On its truth, he tells us,

[4] Meiklejohn: op. cit., p. 266.

he is content to let his whole position stand or fall. "All the activities which give man dignity are done 'for the state.' "[5] This is monstrously false, and its falsity is not in the least mitigated by the proposition which he adds to conciliate the fears of liberals. "The test of any government is found in the dignity and freedom, the equality and independence of its citizens. It exists through and for them, just as they exist through and for it."

There are other dignities than those of the market place and public forum—the dignity of incorruptible pursuit of truth, of the cultivation of friendship, of courage against odds, of shared joys and contained grief. To say that human beings "exist through and for the state" is mystical nonsense whose vicious effects are not likely to be lessened by pious phrases about the state existing "through and for them." No parity can be drawn between these two expressions. In any reasonable and humane philosophy, human personalities are prior to the state, not in the order of time or dependence, but in the order of significance. The alternative which Mr. Meiklejohn sets before us of worshipping either God or the State must be rejected as false. The first may have therapeutic uses for the tender-minded, but the second means worshipping other men or, what is just as bad, ourselves. It is truer and more conducive to human happiness to regard the state as an instrument of social action whose goodness must be judged in relation to the interests of the personalities it affects.

"Interests" are precisely what Mr. Meiklejohn refuses to accept as a principle of understanding or evaluating state action. In consequence, when his discussion actually connects with the world of political realities, it turns out to be an attack upon an attitude which, so long as governments are run by men, we cannot have too much of—namely, intelligent vigilance against abuse of delegated power and against usurpation of authority. The trouble with us Americans, complains Mr.

[5] Ibid., p. 267.

Meiklejohn, is that we have assumed that our public servants "need to be watched, to be kept under constant pressure by us. And the inevitable result is that we have had as public officials the kind of person who needs to be watched, who responds to pressure."[6] And where in this wide world, in which the best intelligence is limited, in which temptation shadows opportunity and power grows on what it feeds, will we find men who do not need to be watched, who can be infallibly relied upon to represent faithfully all groups in the community? The pressure of group interests is one form of participation in democratic government. Instead of deploring it, it should be encouraged to be open, pluralistic, and reasonable.

The most charitable interpretation of Mr. Meiklejohn's position is that he is offering a defense, not of democracy, but of a benevolent dictatorship by those who know what we ought to want better than we know ourselves. But one of the troubles with a benevolent dictatorship, even assuming that it has this remarkable knowledge, is that no one knows how long it will remain benevolent.

It is not true, therefore, that in all circumstances teachers should accept the cultural authority of the group by which the education is given. The objects of their enduring allegiance must include something higher than the authority of clerks and officials, rules of institutions—whether church or state—or even wishes of parents. They will show a decent respect toward them but they cannot permit them to violate the ends of education, as we have described them in our opening chapters, without betraying their trust to their students and their calling as teachers.

[6] Ibid., p. 285.

Chapter 5

AMERICAN SOCIETY AND
EDUCATION

---

*"If we could first know where we are
and whither we are tending, we could
better judge what to do and how to do
it."*   LINCOLN

IF WHAT has been said so far is true, it follows that without
exaggerating the influence of education in a democratic society, without denying the more important role of other social
forces, educators can still play a significant part. What should
their part be? What are the realistic alternatives between
which they must choose with specific reference to the development of American society? The ends of education are not
only guides to teaching activity, they are also criteria by which
the direction of social institutions may be evaluated. If they
are taken seriously, what do they commit us to in the way
of social responsibilities at the present juncture of affairs?
Some historical considerations are relevant in order to provide
a perspective upon these questions.

Both in its failures and in its positive achievements, the history of American education reflects in a distinctive way the
history of American society. In the early centuries of the
American experience the new world imposed a manner of life
upon the settlers which was far different from anything they

had known in Europe. But their ideas about the world, including their ideas about education, were European. In everyday affairs they lived forward; in affairs of the "mind" they thought backwards. They remained colonists of Europe in cultural matters long after they achieved their political independence and began the unique historical career of the American republic. Their schooling was formal, meager, and unrelated to their life problems. Learning, beyond the bare minimum of literacy, was primarily for adornment and polite communication except for those who ultimately went into the professions. It was the home, the farm, the town meeting, and community affairs which bred the habits, attitudes, and values necessary to master the major social experiences.

Gradually, and then at an accelerated pace, the pattern of American economy changed. A largely agricultural community became industrialized and urbanized. By the twentieth century it had been transformed into the foremost capitalist nation on earth. Education now became something that "paid off," if not immediately, then in the "long run." It tied into rapidly multiplying vocational opportunities. The school took the place of the disappearing frontier as an open door to opportunity. The cults of quantity, narrow utility, quick returns, and go-getting, competitive individualism were taken over by the schools from commerce and industry. "Taken" is too strong a word. They were breathed in from an untroubled atmosphere of cumulative material prosperity.

The great American faith in education was justified not only by its material rewards but by fundamental articles in the political credo of American democracy. The founders of the American republic were acutely aware of the twofold danger that beset their new venture—tyrannical usurpation and mob rule. They put their hope in an enlightened citizenry, eternally vigilant against abuses of government. Only education could produce this enlightenment and vigilance. Later, the process of education was conceived as the primary agency of Americanizing the heterogeneous national groups which flocked to these shores from all corners of Europe. The successive waves of immigrants were not completely assimilated—partly because of their own resistance, partly because of the snobbery of the native groups which erected lines of social differentiation along the lines of origin. But all embraced the American faith in education. The newcomers saw in the large educational opportunities offered, a remarkable promise for their children. They were to be given an opportunity to make good, to improve the family station and go as high as their capacity, energy, means, and luck could carry them.

American education to a large measure can be explained in terms of these twin *motifs* of social idealism and material returns. Together with the decentralized character of administration, they explain the traditionalism and flexibility, the social sensitiveness and curricular *chaos* of American education. These, in turn, permitted certain patterns of freedom to develop. With American industry profiting from the fruits of scientific research, hardly any bounds were set to freedom of inquiry in the physical and biological sciences. In time, the inquiring attitude began to seep over into the fields of the social sciences where it encountered some opposition as regional folkways came under critical scrutiny. But there was little in the findings of the social scientists to challenge the basic economic and social mores of the country. Resistance to scientific inquiry, or what passed as such, became episodic. Professional habits and an intellectual timidity before difficult social problems were much more decisive in keeping social scientists in line than overt threats of coercion.

The American economy was pervaded by an unshakable confidence in its eternal stability. It could view with equanimity the talk and programs of scientific activity in the schools and elsewhere, for no live options appeared to which these programs could give a cutting edge. Yet the growth of scientific knowledge was not without influence. Together with the remarkable technological advances in the media of communication, it undermined the blind faith of fundamentalist religion and put it on the defensive.

It was in this period, when American capitalism seemed most stable, that the philosophy of progressive education emerged. As a philosophy it made relatively little headway; but the methods and techniques associated with it were taken over by leading experimental schools, taught in some influential teachers colleges, and introduced in very limited sectors of public education. The new methods and techniques stressed the importance of the voluntary participation of the child in the learning process. They aimed to bring together the method of experimental finding-out and democratic co-operation in solving problems and understanding the world. Presupposing the validity of the democratic ideal, they made the child central in the educational scheme of things. Nonetheless, progressive education existed only on the periphery and in some of the interstices of the public school system.

After 1929 all this changed. The permanent crisis of the American economy began. The specter of depression would never thereafter be banished from the consciousness of even the most sanguine defenders of the existing order. The very sanctity of the capitalist order itself came under attack. In a few years, the theme songs of rugged individualism in both business and education sounded hopelessly out of key in relation to the problems of continuous employment, adequate living standards, and equality of educational opportunity. The ferment of new hopes and ideas spread throughout society. America was drawn more closely into the orbit of international, economic, and political affairs. In the name of capitalism and in its defense, a series of governmental measures were introduced to counteract the excesses of unplanned free enterprise, measures which profoundly modified the legal structure of society. The necessities of government intervention, subvention, and control, as an expression of a tendency towards state capitalism, were greatly intensified by measures taken to prepare for war and to resist fascist aggression. The psychological mind-set of the country altered in consequence of these changes. Exaggerated fears of dictatorship blossomed in some quarters, exaggerated hopes for a revolution by consent in others. Traditional political labels no longer signified what they once had. The composite picture was one of confusion unframed by any clear lines of policy.

American education followed in the wake of these changes. It offered no leadership and no one looked to it for leadership. Where it was not passive, its role was strictly defensive. The primary concerns of school systems throughout the country, in the years subsequent to 1929, were problems connected with the physical survival of the educational plant, the retention of personnel, and the riding out of a campaign of retrenchment. Educational thinking in most institutions went on a prolonged *ad hoc* basis. Educational practices—because of the urgency, first of economic need, then of rearmament, and finally of war—became more and more narrowly vocational.

There were two notable changes in the field of educational philosophy. One was the clarification of the progressive philosophy of education and its social reorientation; the other was the emergence of an anti-secular philosophy which sought to find a unifying faith for democracy in a metaphysics or religion, which, beginning with the reformation of the schools, would end with the transformation of the social order—or in its more recent version, beginning with the reformation of society, would transform education.

The philosophy of progressive education had from the outset been committed to the belief that only in a democracy, and in a continuously expanding social democracy, can the end of individual growth be achieved. This follows from the concern with which the needs of every child were to be considered, the necessity of harmonizing these needs to permit their fruitful expansion, and the recognition that genuine equality of educational opportunity demands social democracy at one end and industrial democracy at the other. But such a philosophy obviously could not be implemented on a large scale in a stable class society, if only because its economic costs would be prohibitive from the point of view of the pecuniary standard of real estate tax boards which watched school budgets with suspicious eyes. Although such a philosophy could do something, even in a truncated form, to improve existing practices, in order to effect fundamental changes it would have to be harnessed to a progressive social philosophy and movement which had not yet emerged as a national force.

Yet the teaching practices which flowed from the central philosophy of progressive education, when properly understood, were so inherently reasonable and, when intelligently introduced, so beneficial to the young, that they appealed to many who had no concern or interest in the premises from which they were originally derived. Some of these practices, as has been noted, found their way into public school systems. But for many reasons, the progressive schoolroom practices made their greatest strides in private experimental schools. It was in these schools, supported by intelligent middle-class groups anxious to see the best in their children developed, that progressive education evolved its most distinctive techniques and projects. Yet it was precisely among these groups that the social implications of progressive education were disregarded, or treated as phraseological pieties. Progressive education became a kind of luxury for the intelligent well-to-do parents looking for better schools. These schools took the democratic philosophy of progressive education for granted. They introduced it only in the political contexts of their curriculum, and wherever class activities were entrusted to students themselves. But as a social philosophy with a pressing relevance to questions of social organization it was largely ignored.[1]

[1] Cf. George S. Counts: *Dare the Schools Build a New Social Order?* (New York: John Day Co.; 1932).

The great divide in progressive education occurred after the depression. The theoretical leaders of the movement, with few exceptions, in evaluating the work of the experimental progressive schools criticized them for neglecting to relate the content of their activity, wherever it was relevant, to the democratic philosophy. They did not object to the child-centered school, but warned that without social reference such schools would produce egocentric children lacking allegiance to tested ideals. Without tying the progressive philosophy to any *specific* social and political program, they tried to link it up with the great task of democratizing American culture.

To many professed followers of progressive education, this came as a rude awakening. They had committed themselves to a system of pedagogy, not to a social philosophy. They began to see that, even as a pedagogy, progressive education already involved a commitment to democracy—a totalitarian culture could use few, if any, of its techniques of doubt, challenge, inquiry, and test in the classroom—and that this commitment was so wholehearted that it went far beyond the limits of conventional democracy. As leading progressive educators identified themselves with the social and political struggles for democracy, both inside and outside the schools, their rank and file following, particularly among middle-class groups, fell away. This defection was reinforced by a group of educators who had substituted a paternalistic conception of welfare for the vision of democratic mutualism and political liberty central to progressive education. Having sold their birthright of American freedom for a pot of Russian message, they regarded education as a process in which the minds of the young were to be stuffed with salvationary doctrines about the Coming Day. Some of them ended up by denouncing progressive education as a "petty-bourgeois reformist deviation," and the philosophy of Dewey as a refined expression of American imperialism.

The consequence was that the philosophy underlying progressive education was stripped to fighting weight, and was challenged to restate its position in such a way that what formerly had been presupposed was now explicitly stated.

Before the philosophy of progressive education could reformulate its fundamental ideas, it was placed on the defensive by the pedagogical scares generated by postwar Soviet political and technological triumphs. These developments have been considered in Chapter One.

When we speak of the role educators should play in society or of the social choices they must make, it is necessary to introduce a distinction to avoid radical misunderstanding. This distinction is between the choice of social philosophies educators adopt as citizens, and their educational choices as teachers seeking to discover the curriculums and procedures relevant to the making of intelligent decisions on social philosophies by students. The two are related but by no means identical. The first is a conclusion warranted by evidence easily available to other citizens, as well as by special considerations that appeal to educators in the light of their professional concern. The second involves a series of difficult and delicate tasks of educational discovery. Its fulfillment must respect the integrity of individual students' minds and help them grow to maturity, while at the same time seeking to impart the knowledge, skills, and values without which intelligent and responsible choice is impossible. The first question—choice of a social philosophy —I shall discuss briefly in the remainder of this chapter; the second, the main educational task, in subsequent chapters.

The fundamental social problem of our culture—fundamental in the sense that it conditions a satisfactory solution of all other important social problems—is to defend and extend our democratic heritage of rights and freedoms in an industrial economy that can provide security for all. That security, on a plane commensurate with standards of human dignity, has nowhere in the world been achieved in an unplanned economy.

Nor has it ever been achieved by a planned economy under a political dictatorship. For if political freedom without economic security is defective and precarious, economic security without political democracy is impossible. Slaves have no security when their masters possess absolute power over them.

Despite the rhetorical invocations to free enterprise by almost all groups in American life, including some who do not believe in it, an examination of what they concretely propose in order to reverse the trend toward economic centralization and government control shows that in effect the movement towards a corporate economy, private or collective or mixed, is regarded as irreversible. A social scheme in which a government agency *planfully* encourages or strengthens a sector of private economy in relation to the total economy is obviously not one of free enterprise. The genuine issue lies in another dimension. Shall our corporate economy—indeed, *can* our corporate economy—function within a democratic framework of control, or does its logic of production require some authoritarian cultural order to supervene upon what we have known until now? Shall the end of the free market in commodities spell the end of the free market in ideas?

To say that this great decision is *ours* to make already entails the rejection of the simple economic determinism shared alike by doctrinaire orthodox Marxists and their equally doctrinaire opponents, of whom H. J. Laski and F. A. Hayek are representative.[2] It involves a philosophy of history according to which the mode of economic production does not always uniquely determine the political and moral quality of a society, although it always has a pervasive conditioning effect. It involves a philosophy of culture according to which, within

[2] This characterization of Laski refers to the position he took in his latter-day writings, particularly his *Reflections on the Revolution of Our Time* (New York: The Viking Press; 1943) and *Faith, Reason, and Civilization* (New York: The Viking Press; 1944). Cf. my analysis of the former in *Partisan Review*, Vol. 10, No. 5 (September-October 1943), pp. 442–7.

limits, human beings *may* redetermine the direction of their social development.

The arguments against control of our corporate economy in the interest of private profit rather than of public welfare have filled volumes. But they can be synoptically classified under five heads. I cite them not so much to prove a case as to indicate the variety of considerations which enter into the evaluation of the problem and the rich curricular material they suggest for exploration.

(a) the argument from utility and efficiency. A profit economy fails to use natural and social resources efficiently. It is a wasteful social system—wasteful through its pillaging of the nation's natural resources, through enforced idleness of men and machines, often through failure to employ the best known technology. This waste is as irretrievable as it is socially unwise. Yet most of it is unavoidable in a profit economy.

(b) the argument from security—economic, psychological, and political. Periodic crises of mounting intensity are indigenous to our existing economy. The resulting distress and unemployment, even when mitigated by social welfare legislation, generate deep emotional disturbances and maladjustments. Chronic fears, worries, and resentments seek unhealthy outlets. A mass base is prepared for totalitarian movements. Those who suffer tend to dismiss the ideals of freedom as empty; those who enjoy comfort and power tend to abridge them out of fear.

(c) the argument from morality. In our existing economy, service to the community is instrumental—often only incidental—to profit, which recognizes no essential social responsibility. Competitive attitudes are built up which regard human beings in industrial and other social relations as tools, not as fellow-members in a community of shared interests. "The relationship between person and person," Felix Adler rightly says, "is mankind's supreme concern." Where a profit economy does not systematically deteriorate the quality of this relationship, it operates in independence of it.

(d) the argument from culture. The arts and sciences, and in a more literal sense their practitioners, are often compelled to serve as handmaids to business and corporate wealth. The quality of public taste, particularly in the fields of the popular arts and communication, is degraded by standards of commercialism. In consequence, mass culture tends to crowd out high culture.

(e) the argument from democracy. Because capital means not only power over things but power over men, concentrations of economic power in the hands of a few result in great social inequalities and in disproportionate political influence of different social groups in the community. The cumulative consequences of the functioning of an unplanned economy make a mockery of the ideal of equal opportunity.

These considerations, even if their validity is apparent to all citizens, by themselves are not sufficient to establish the desirability of a planned welfare economy. For if the present state of affairs is bad, it does not follow that what is proposed to succeed it will be better. It may be worse. But, before stating the other side of the case, there are some further observations, bound up with the professional activity of educators, that strengthen the argument for a welfare economy.

The first is the obvious fact that, in our present society, the hardships and dislocations produced by depressions have a pernicious effect upon the conditions of the educator's life—his freedom, security, earnings, and social status. In a lesser measure, shortsighted financial control of budgets in normal periods leads to similar results. Together, they prevent the proper expansion of educational facilities, the recruiting of superior men and women into the profession, and the introduction on a wide scale of methods and techniques devised by the best pedagogic wisdom.

Second, it is notoriously true that large numbers of our
young men and women are deprived of the higher reaches of
education to which their capacities entitle them. And not only
of the higher reaches.[3] This is a loss to the community as much
as to the individuals concerned. Nor can the situation be rem-
edied altogether by free tuition scholarships. The deprivations
some students' families incur by paying for living expenses, not
to speak of the loss of earning power, are important elements
in determining whether they are to continue their education.
Equal educational opportunity to develop the potential gifts
and aptitudes of all individuals, often asserted to be one of the
cornerstones of American democracy, cannot be easily realized
in our economy without massive government support.

Third and most important of all, there is an ever-growing
separation between the work of the liberal arts schools in help-
ing students find and mature their powers, and the vocational
opportunities society provides for their exercise. Here we are
confronted by a major educational problem which cannot be
solved until the educational system becomes a co-operative part
of the social economy. All available evidence points to the
fact that, so far as the performance of the country's work is
concerned, many of those who have received a liberal education will be "overeducated." There will be no room for them.
As the compulsory school age increases, as ambitious scholarship plans and government subsidies go into effect, as successive spins of the economic cycle make school a more attractive
alternative than idling on the streets, the number of college-
trained men and women will vastly increase even if they do not
include all who should go to college. There are not enough
positions in industry and the professions to absorb them in
work commensurate with their talents.

[3] For an interesting and informative treatment of the subject, cf. W. L.
Warner, R. J. Havighurst, and M. B. Loeb: *Who Shall Be Educated?
The Challenge of Unequal Opportunities* (New York: Harper &
Brothers; 1944).

It is extremely unlikely that most human beings will be content if they have to labor at tasks that make no call upon the capacities of perception, imagination, judgment, and insight which a liberal education presumably develops. The consequence may very well be a white-collared proletariat, dissatisfied when it is employed, embittered when it is not, and inflammable to appeals that promise an illusory larger field for talents.

To some extent the situation will be alleviated by reduction in the hours of work and the resulting multiplication of vocational opportunities. But there is no reason to believe that, as technological developments continue, the number of positions requiring the skills and capacities of well-educated individuals will increase. The future opens the vista of a deep educational cleft in our cultural life: on the one hand, vocational opportunities whose fulfillment for the great majority has nothing to do with their educational preparation; on the other, leisure time spent as a release from boredom and monotony. This perpetuates the divorce between "earning one's living" and "living one's life," between meaningless drudgery "on the job" and a significant life "after hours," which is one of the powerful sources both of externalism and sentimentalism in American life. Adult education can do something to fill the void at the beginning; but the more serious and successful it is, the more poignant becomes the awareness of this educational dualism.

If the school is to serve society, society should serve the school. Educators cannot with good conscience remain indifferent to a spectacle in which eager and capable youths, on whom they have lavished years of careful teaching, are turned adrift to find what places they can in an economy that may not need them. The school should help find the opportunities in which they can prove themselves. It should become an integral part of the planning agencies of the future. Educators must move into the forefront of social and economic planning to represent an interest which is of pre-eminent public importance.

Others may keep a special eye on the production of wealth or the efficiency of organization; the educators must never lose sight of *persons* as they are affected in and by the production of wealth and the functioning of organization. However else social engineering is conceived, it must also be conceived as an opportunity to create opportunities for significant work. Such a conception requires the profound modification of a social system in which economic profit and loss are the strongest directing principles.

The arguments against planned social control of our economy are not many. But they make up in power for what they lack in number. They reduce themselves to one central contention. Planned control of society in the nature of the case must lead to such monopolistic concentrations of power—economic, legal, and educational—in the hands of a few planners that political freedom and all other freedoms enshrined in our Bill of Rights will disappear. It is not the state that will wither away but democracy. An unplanned economy *may* end up in totalitarianism; a planned economy *must*.

As the argument works itself out, it is based on two impressive lines of evidence. The first attempts to prove by an analysis of planning and the nature of its centralized controls that no significant choices can be left open to any but a few individuals if the economy is to function. Political sanctions must accompany every decision of the master-planners who thereby become the masters of our destiny. De Maistre said that at the foundation of all society stands the executioner; Hayek says in a planned society he inhabits its every room. The second line of evidence is historical. It points out that nations like Nazi Germany and Communist Russia, in which economic planning has been introduced on a large scale, are absolute dictatorships —in effect, gigantic concentration camps ruled by a secret police. If either form of the argument is valid, it would constitute more than a sufficient reply to all proposals for a planned society, especially in the eyes of educators. For education in such a system is nothing but an elaborate apparatus for conditioning slaves to the efficient performance of their rounds and duties.

For present purposes I am interested in showing the educational implications of this issue rather than arguing for a conclusion.[4] But in evaluating the strength of the two lines of evidence against a planned society, it is clear that the historical argument is the weaker of the two. In all totalitarian cultures, democratic liberties were *first* destroyed and only then was a planned economy introduced under the aegis of a dictatorship. Where a planned economy is introduced into a country with strong democratic traditions, the historical comparisons, although instructive, are not decisive. It is the analytical argument which has the strongest force. There is what Lewis Corey has aptly called a "totalitarian potential" in the structure of a planned economy which, if realized, would mean the rule of an iron-clad dictatorship. But a planned economy, as we have seen, has a libertarian potential too, because it can liberate productive forces for a more abundant life for all. Which one becomes actual is not a question of historical destiny or inevitable law, but of human decision which will fall one way or the other depending upon what scientific knowledge and moral courage those who are pledged to democracy bring to

[4] For further discussion of this issue, cf. Ludwig von Mises: *Socialism* (New York: The Macmillan Company; 1937) and *Omnipotent Government* (New Haven: Yale University Press; 1944), and F. A. Hayek: *The Road to Serfdom* (Chicago: University of Chicago Press; 1944), in opposition to a planned society; and, in favor, Lewis Corey: *The Unfinished Task* (New York: The Macmillan Company; 1942) and Abba Lerner: *The Economics of Control* (New York: The Macmillan Company; 1945). Also my article, "The Moral Force of Socialism," Max Eastman's critique, "Can a Planned Society Be Democratic?" and my rejoinder, "Freedom and Socialism," in *The New Leader*, 1944 and 1945. These are reprinted in my *Political Power and Personal Freedom* (New York: Criterion Books; 1959) together with several other studies in behalf of a democratic socialist society.

bear on it. *A planned economy need not be total, and it may operate under plural forms of participation and control.*

The experience of Great Britain, although not decisive, weighs very heavily against the analysis of Professor Hayek and others who conclude that the road to socialization is a one-way road to industrial serfdom. For under the Labour government Great Britain carried out an extensive program of national ownership of means of production without in any way affecting the structure of civil rights and freedoms. The English experience is instructive in other ways. It shows that socialization as a principle need not be an all-or-none affair, that where problems of social ownership or control arise, it is a question of more or less rather than either-or. This has been accepted even by non-socialist regimes. The Tory party in displacing the Labour party in political power retained most of the socialized sector of industry and indeed prided itself on the fact that its program of public housing went even farther. The English experience certainly revealed that socialization was not an economic panacea, that at best it is a means toward a set of ends defined as a society of free and richly endowed human beings. But it also revealed just as conclusively that, so long as the political processes of democracy are not eroded, socialization in itself constitutes no threat. This view is reinforced by the discovery that social control can be exercised in ways other than by outright social ownership. Indeed, from the point of view of the worker on the job, some sense of active participation in determining the conditions and rewards of work seems more important than the forms of ownership. Workers know that they can be economically exploited just as much by the state as by private employers. This means that decisions on what to socialize, when, and by what institutional devices must be decided with an eye not alone to increasing production but also to improving the quality of human relationships.

To the historical warning that a planned economy has hitherto functioned only within a totalitarian framework can be counterposed the historical reminder that it was out of the consequences of an unplanned economy that this totalitarian framework arose. To the analysis that planning cannot function without political dictatorship can be counterposed the analysis that an unplanned economy cannot function without breeding want, unemployment, and the danger of war. How can the issue be resolved without leaving it to the chances of drift or tragic civil upheaval? Is there any common ground?

The arguments of both sides presuppose the common ground of a democratic ethos. This offers a basis for inquiry, for discussion and experiment, and for possible resolution of conflict. Does one believe in the democratic right of equal opportunity? What measures of social control will establish the positive conditions without which it is an empty phrase? Does one advocate a specific measure of socialization? How does it affect the democratic rights we wish to preserve? Does one democratic right clash with another in certain situations? How do their respective fulfillments or frustrations affect the cluster of other democratic rights to which both profess agreement? The process stops and begins again as problem follows problem. Decisions alter the conditions which provoked the challenge, and their consequences give birth to new challenges and predicaments in an unending series of social problems. In a sense, it is the *way* this series of social problems is met that constitutes *the* social problem which is also *the* political problem and *the* moral problem of our age.

This provides the clue to the vocation of the school in the American community and, when a world government is achieved, in the international community as well. Its function is to serve as a common *institutional* ground in which are forged those attitudes of reasonableness, of scientific inquiry, and of devotion to shared human values which must underlie all differences within a democratic culture if it is to survive. Where churches and sects and nations divide, and in some respects men will always be divided, the schools can unite by becoming the temples and laboratories of a common democratic faith.

Educators, like all other citizens, cannot avoid taking a position on the central issues on which men divide. But their task as educators is not to preach any solutions they hold as citizens. Their duty is so to teach that, on the appropriate levels, students become aware of the central issues of their culture, habituated to scientific inquiry into the consequences of proposed solutions, sensitive to the values involved in these solutions and affected by them, and courageous in accepting the conclusions to which method and insight lead. We shall soon see what this means in the way of curriculums and teaching procedures. But before going on I wish to repudiate as explicitly as I can a fantastic caricature of the notion that educators should relate their teaching to the basic problems of their culture. According to this caricature, educators must subscribe to the true social philosophy, socialist, capitalist, or whatever label is affixed to it, before they can be qualified to teach; and the educational system must adopt a curriculum that will help achieve a specific political program.[5]

What *is* being asserted is that the materials and methods that are relevant to the intelligent determination of a social philosophy for our age should pervade the curriculum, that the education of citizens of a democracy requires not exclusive, but central, emphasis on focal problems of our culture and the

[5] A crass illustration of this misrepresentation is contained in the remarks of William Dighton in *Current History*, Vol. 6, No. 34 (June 1944), pp. 473–90. Referring to my criticism of Mark van Doren's *Liberal Education* in *Partisan Review*, Vol. 11, No. 2 (Spring 1944), pp. 161–7, he writes: "Professor Hook can find no place in his ideology for the St. John's program even in one institution, and since a return to the classics and religion is reactionary, presumably he would have them universally banned because they are detrimental to the establishment of the socialist state." There are four errors of fact and one false inference in this sentence.

intellectual skills and moral habits with which to cope with them. Agreement on conclusions is not a precondition of agreement on what is relevant in reaching them.

So much the citizens of a democracy have the right to expect of the educators in a democracy. On these basic questions of curriculum orientation there are no educational experts. But when we ask: what concretely is involved in the construction of such a curriculum? what should the order and weight of its studies be? shall all, part, or none of it be prescribed for everybody? what teaching methods should be employed? what is the nature of indoctrination and what should its role be? shall vocational study be separated from liberal study? what is a good teacher and how shall he be selected?—we are asking questions which the professional educator is best qualified to answer.

The answers to these questions today are varied and conflicting. But discussion and experiment can show that some are better than others. Where answers express world-views independently of our existing educational problems, it is unlikely that a consensus can be established. But insofar as we take as our starting point democratic ideals, irrespective of their different philosophical underpinnings, we can fruitfully explore their curricular consequences. In their light, we may even broaden the area of philosophical agreement.

Chapter 6

THE CONTENT OF
EDUCATION

---

*"Finding the material for learning within
experience is only the first step. The
next step is the progressive development
of what is already experienced into a
fuller and richer and more organized
form, that gradually approximates the
form in which subject-matter is presented
to the skilled, mature person."*

JOHN DEWEY

ALL CONTROVERSIES in education start from dissatisfaction with
what our children are learning or with what they are not
being taught. *What should we teach and why?* is a question
that arises on the very threshold of intelligent concern with
the process of schooling. It is a sad commentary on the character of contemporary education that few institutions, until
the war brought an unsought leisure to liberal arts teachers,
stopped to ask themselves this question; and that still fewer
were able to answer it when they did. To be sure, it is not the
only question that can or should be answered, nor is it unrelated to other questions of great import like: *Whom are we
educating?* and *For what are we educating?* But it has a direct-
ness and a challenging simplicity that everyone recognizes and

which no philosophy of education that seeks to guide practice can evade.

Past and Present

The easiest answer to the question *What should we teach?* is also the most deceptive. We should teach—so runs this answer—those subjects which embody the great truths of our human tradition, the accumulated knowledge, skills, and wisdom which are the inalienable heritage of every child. This answer is deceptive because it assumes that there are educators, or others for that matter, who assert that we should *not* teach these things. If there are any such, they have never given a sign of their presence. To infer that those who believe that *more* than these things should be taught are therefore opposed to including them is to exhibit one of those passionate lapses in thinking which suggest that the issue lies somewhere else. The answer is deceptive because it is an over-all truism through which is insinuated the notion that emphasis upon *present-day problems* involves its rejection or denial. Nothing can be taught which does not at one point or another involve the use of some tradition—let it be no more than language. Nothing can be learned which is not continuous with something already known. Instead of an honest confrontation of the issue: What should be the *relative* place of study of the past and present in our education? the issue is lost in the rhetorical flourishes and overtones of what in Aristotle's day was already recognized as a commonplace.

Nor is the issue fairly stated by those who, like Hutchins and Maritain, charge modern educators with the fallacy of "presentism." According to the former, those who would include a study of modern industrial processes in the education of the American student are adherents of "the cult of immediacy." "In this view the way to comprehend the world is to grapple with the reality you find about you. . . . There is no past."[1] One would imagine that grappling with the realities that surround us is precisely the way to begin to understand the world. One would imagine that through such an effort we would discover not only that there is a past, but that it has an inescapable bearing and importance upon the realities surrounding us. To identify the view that the present world is a legitimate object of study for those who are going to live in it, with the view that the present is nothing but a specious bloom of immediacy with no roots in the past and no fruits in the future, is intellectually cheap. It evades considered argument by caricature, and blocks fruitful discussion of the place of the present *and* past in a desirable educational experience.

There is a certain ambiguity in the term "present" which must be clarified before we ask whether our education is to be oriented toward the past or present. In one sense all education is *for* the present. That is to say, the justification for teaching or learning anything must be its observable consequences within our experience. Whatever other world an individual will inhabit, his life will be spent in this one. Whatever may be the society of the future, either it will be continuous with the society in which he now lives or it will develop out of its conflicts and problems.

Whatever we teach, whether it be a tale of glory, the procession of the seasons, or the mystery of the atom, we teach ultimately for the sake of the present. We teach our children reading, writing, and arithmetic not because they are skills that were once acquired by man—there have been many skills developed in the past that were better forgotten—but because they have a *continuing function of a desirable nature in the present world*. Reference to the present is inescapable no matter what interests or powers we would awaken, no matter what knowledge we would impart. Whitehead, who is often

[1] Robert M. Hutchins: *Education for Freedom* (Baton Rouge: Louisiana State University Press; 1943), p. 32.

invoked to justify educational practices he in fact condemns, states the point with unusual eloquence.

> The only use of a knowledge of the past is to equip us for the present. No more deadly harm can be done to young minds than by depreciation of the present. The present contains all that there is. It is holy ground; for it is the past; and it is the future. At the same time it must be observed that an age is no less past if it existed two hundred years ago than if it existed two thousand years ago. Do not be deceived by the pedantry of dates. The ages of Shakespeare and of Molière are no less past than are the ages of Sophocles and of Virgil. The communion of saints is a great and inspiring assemblage, but it has only one possible hall of meeting, and that is, the present; and the mere lapse of time through which any particular group of saints must travel to reach that meeting-place, makes very little difference.[2]

To say that the present is sacred ground does not imply that the problems and materials of present-day life are sacred. For the present in this context designates the locus of educational justification, not the nature of educational subject matter. But at the same time it does suggest a criterion which will enable us to evaluate the respective claims of different subject matters. This is the criterion of *relevance*.

To demand that the content of instruction be relevant to the present emphatically does not preclude a study of the past. It only prevents us from getting lost in the past. It enables us to make some intelligent *selection* out of the limitless materials inherited from the past.

The facile use of over-simple disjunctions is the bane of educational discussion. Posing the problem as if we must choose *between* a total present-day curriculum or a total classical curriculum is the worst illustration of this use. No one can construct a curriculum out of the material of the past without

[2] Alfred North Whitehead: *The Organization of Thought* (Philadelphia: J. B. Lippincott Co.; 1918), pp. 6–7.

some implicit reference to the present: no one can address himself to the problems of today without considering the world of our yesterdays. The genuine issue is where the *emphasis* should fall, and what the degree of *explicitness* should be in relating the past to the present.

To what in the present should the content of study be relevant? In the broadest sense of the term, to the fundamental *problems* of the age—to the social, political, intellectual, and, if we like, the spiritual questions posed by our time and culture. Here the issue acquires a biting edge. It is these problems, problems which will not be denied even if we refuse to study them, that should serve as the chief subject matters around which to build educational instruction. By "chief" subject matters I mean not merely that at a certain point in schooling they become the focal problems of study, but that they become the points of departure for *planning* the content of curriculum at other levels, too. Far from unduly narrowing the course of study, we shall see that such orientation expands and enriches it without converting it into an archaic or contemporary miscellany.

The reason this approach enriches the course of study is twofold. First, the past world and the present are so continuous that there are few problems which can be intelligently understood without transcending the immediate context in which they are discovered. Second, the nature of present-day problems is such that they require the mastery of certain subject matters and techniques which are themselves not problematic, and which have no *direct* relation to these problems. The first reason explains why the study of the present must be included in the education of modern man. For it provides the key to what to include and exclude from the past. The second reason explains why the mastery of certain skills and areas of knowledge must be given precedence over that of others in the organization of a curriculum: why, for example, an ability to read critically is more important than an ability to typewrite;

why knowledge of the essential elements of statistics should be more generally required than knowledge of the history of astronomy. Together, these reasons explain, as we shall see, what elements in education should be constant and what not; how curriculums may be intelligently changed in content and emphasis; how they may be different and yet equally good at different times.

There is a way of understanding the doctrine of relevance according to which it is the quintessence of an "anti-educational" attitude. "Relevance" here becomes the pretext under which every passing whim, fancy, or predicament in the social scene stakes a claim for inclusion in the curriculum of studies. The attempt to make education relevant is construed by Mr. Wriston, former president of Brown University, as necessitating overnight revisions of the educational curriculum, and roundly condemned. "The doctrine of relevance is valid only in a perfectly stable world where the future is easily predictable. . . ." But such a world is impossible. Therefore it is a fundamental error to organize a course of study whose consequence is "shallow concentration upon transitory environmental circumstances."[3]

Once more, the injection of an over-simple disjunction burkes genuine issues. Either the world is perfectly stable or it travels like mad! Study must either be profound or shallow! Presumably the past is never studied shallowly or the present profoundly! But these are absurd alternatives. The fundamental problems of an age are not born overnight, nor are they ever solved in a fortnight. They are not disasters before which we are helpless, nor are they business opportunities which we must snatch before they disappear. Education relevant to an understanding of the place of war in modern society is not an education relevant specifically to Pearl Harbor or to the next occasion of war. An education relevant to an understanding of

[3] Theodore M. Greene, *et. al.*: *Liberal Education Re-Examined* (New York: Harper & Brothers; 1943), pp. 9–11.

economic depressions, their causes and control, is not relevant to selling long or short on the stock market. An education relevant to understanding the problems of preserving peace and freedom in a nuclear age will not equip us to fathom the latest maneuvers of the Soviet representatives at the disarmament table in Geneva. The problem of reconciling social security and political democracy was not created by the New Deal, nor was the problem of racial conflict created by Hitler. To speak intelligently of *fundamental* problems is at the same time to distinguish between them and *ephemeral* problems. The *specific* form a fundamental problem may take will vary from situation to situation. But recognizing that it is a specific form of a *fundamental* problem is a genuine educational discovery. It is a discovery that immediately lifts the problem out of ephemeral detail, and without losing sight of its dramatic significance for the present, uncovers the connections with the past and the possible bearings on the future which are of its very nature.

Let us examine some concrete illustrations of contemporary problems and issues, so despised by traditionalists, in order to see what would be involved in their adequate understanding. Nothing is more contemporary than present-day totalitarianism in its various forms. Can its nature be understood without a social and economic analysis of capitalism and its periodic cycles? Can we come to grips with its rationalizations, and understand our own minds in relation to it, without some study of the ideas of men like Chamberlain, Nietzsche, Hegel, Rousseau, Locke, Hobbes, Aquinas, Aristotle, and Plato? Can theories of race and racial supremacy be exposed without a sound knowledge of biology and some familiarity with the elements of scientific method? Can an intelligent analysis be made of proposals that the West disarm unilaterally in the belief that the Soviet Union will follow suit, without a study of the pacts and treaties previously entered into by the Kremlin—and the score of their fulfillment? What better texts can be found for an analysis of propaganda and loose writing and thinking, than key pages from Hitler's *Mein Kampf*—or, for that matter, the writings of Russian apologists who argue that the U.S. is not a "true" democracy and that Russia, with a minority one-party dictatorship and absolutely no civil rights for those who disagree with it, is a democracy in a "higher" sense?

Or take a prosaic theme like taxation. Properly approached, it is an exciting introduction not only to questions of economic theory but to principles of social philosophy and theories of government. The problem of conservation of natural resources opens doorways into almost all the sciences. Whatever we touch that is of great moment in the modern world—whether it be urbanization, population trends and housing, unemployment, social security, civil rights and duties, the growth of administrative law, the control of the air, the role of the state, individual enterprise and trade-unions in industry, the origins and proposed cures of war, the promise and dangers of socialism, the prospects of a world state, the sources of racial and religious conflicts—cannot be adequately grasped without exploring the causal and ideational lines that radiate from them to ideas and events in the past. They cannot be studied as they should be without some knowledge of systematic disciplines. And they cannot be pursued for long without discovering the moral commitments we bring to them, and test in the bringing. To fail to realize any one of these truths is a failure of imagination. To fail in carrying home these truths in the practice of the classroom is a failure of pedagogic verve and skill. It is one thing to recognize this failure of imagination and verve in much of contemporary educational procedure. It is quite another thing to build an educational philosophy on the basis of these defects and turn away from present-day problems.

What, indeed, shall we turn to? If we examine the actual content of courses of study based upon material of the past, we make an interesting discovery. A considerable portion of the classical curriculum is devoted to the social and political questions of antiquity, the medieval period, the Renaissance and post-Renaissance—in short, of every age but our own. Those who fulminate against the degeneration of modern education because some schools pay attention to the bridges, waterways, and sanitation systems of our large cities, together with other great feats of engineering, regard it as perfectly proper to study and glow about the marvels of Roman aqueducts, plumbing, and roads. Those who scoff at concern with unemployment and with the devices of ballyhoo by which modern dictators come to power, claim that there is a great lesson to be learned from the role of "bread and circuses" in Roman history. Study of the First and Second World Wars need not be part of a liberal education: the study of the Peloponnesian and Punic Wars must be. The "proper" subject matter of a liberal education, on this view, is not the Russian Revolution but the conspiracy of Cataline; not the state papers of Woodrow Wilson, of Clemenceau, of Lenin, but the orations of Demosthenes and Cicero.

The significance of the fact that the Greeks, the greatest of the ancient peoples, made their history and conducted their education without models, without historical examples, without great books, is lost sight of by those who glorify past times. This does not mean that we can or should imitate the Greeks in this respect. Rather does it suggest that, without denying their legacy, we would do well to add to it in order to leave a still richer patrimony to those who follow us. In education as in life we must learn to look to ourselves as ancestors, not merely descendants.

It is sometimes asserted that present-day social studies must occupy a subordinate place in the curriculum because they do not provide "an intelligible set of organizing principles." What is an intelligble set of organizing principles? Whatever it is, why is it more applicable to the social problems of the past than to those of the present? Can it be argued that in earlier ages men possessed *knowledge* of human affairs, whereas we are misled by *opinion?* This is certainly not the case in other areas of study, particularly the natural sciences. If by an "intelligible set of organizing principles" is meant a standpoint of approach or frame of reference which relates problems to each other and indicates a common mode of analyzing them, then we have such principles in democracy and scientific method. The assumption lurking behind criticisms of this type is that there are no genuine solutions—at least no known solutions—of these acute problems; and that therefore their study must result at best in talk or in an exchange of prejudiced sentiment. Little would be left in the curriculum besides mathematics and science if we were to demand that only problems which can be definitively solved should be taught. But the demand is unreasonable. Intelligent study of social problems is possible even if it generates other problems, even if no more can be seen than that some solutions are inadequate, even if judgment must be suspended. I am *not* saying that no social problems are soluble, for many of them are. I am saying that they warrant study even when no conclusion is warranted.

When the discussion of present or past orientation of curriculum reaches the level of argument a shift commonly takes place. The present is no longer derided, but it is asserted that the best way to approach it is by way of the past. The past is studied not for its own sake, not out of antiquarian interest, not to be imitated, but to be used in understanding the world we live in. It is certainly conceivable that we can get the American student to understand his world by concentrating on Greece, Rome, and medieval society, with a little thrown in from each century except the twentieth. Alexander Meiklejohn has vehemently defended St. John's College, whose curriculum is militantly non-modern, precisely on these grounds.[4] Such claims are always to be welcomed even if they are made to outflank criticisms. For they introduce empirical considerations

[4] Alexander Meiklejohn: "Reply to John Dewey," *Fortune*, Vol. 31, No. 1 (January 1945), p. 207.

that enable us to settle them. In this case, the empirical considerations are so obvious that the claim can be dismissed as of little value. List a dozen of the outstanding features and problems of the modern world. Would they be better understood by studying the culture of Greece and Rome than by studying them directly, introducing the study of the past *only* at those points where the analysis disclosed the past to be *relevant*? Is it a virtue of a curriculum in which modern social philosophies are *not* studied that students, by immersing themselves in the culture of the fifth century B.C., may learn that Roosevelt was not a Communist, and that the W. P. A. had its uses?[5] What a long way 'round to go!

There is only one assumption that makes sense of the apparent paradox of ignoring present-day problems for past-day problems, and of the apparent absurdity of claiming that the study of the past is the best way to understand a present which is itself not studied firsthand. This assumption is that the true answers to our most important problems can best be found by assaying the heritage of the past, that the tradition which gave rise to the classical curriculum is a great storehouse of eternal truths which provide, if not the final, then the most satisfactory answers to the perennial problems of human life and destiny.

All disciplines have a history, but it is not always the case that knowledge of the history of a discipline is necessary for its adequate grasp. The humanities, and in lesser measure the social studies, are essentially historical. If they are taught independently of their historical contexts, except for certain branches of economics, they appear to be thin and skimpy. But

[5] John Tunis in the eleventh of a series of thirteen coast-to-coast radio broadcasts over MBS, under the auspices of Education for Freedom, Inc. The other speakers in the series were Mark van Doren, Robert M. Hutchins, Joseph A. Brandt, Scott Buchanan, Pitirim Sorokin, John U. Nef, Alfred Noyes, The Reverend Robert I. Gannon, S. J., Mortimer Adler, Alexander Meiklejohn, Stringfellow Barr, and John Erskine. For a digest of these addresses and a commentary on them, cf. my review, "Thirteen Arrows Against Liberal Education," *The Humanist*, Vol. 4, new series, No. 1 (Spring 1944), p. 1.

all disciplines of a mathematical and natural scientific character can be effectively mastered without a study of their history. The history of mathematics and science is, of course, a legitimate and valuable study of great cultural significance but it cannot serve as a substitute, or even as a fruitful approach, to the mastery of contemporary mathematics and science, if only because some knowledge of the latter is already presupposed if the history itself is to be intelligible. That is why the proposal of the architects of the St. John's College curriculum that science and mathematics be studied through the reading of the great scientific and mathematical books of the past instead of through the use of adequate contemporary textbooks strikes one as odd and doctrinaire.

One of the more startling innovations of the St. John's curriculum is the prescribed reading of the historical classics in mathematics and science. The works of Euclid and Ptolemy, Kepler and Newton, Galen and Harvey are studied instead of modern systematic textbooks in mathematics, physics, and biology. Nothing indicates so eloquently the dogma-ridden character of the curriculum than this approach to mathematics and the natural sciences. For in *these* disciplines, it is no exaggeration—nor does it betoken lack of piety—to say that the best contributions of the best minds can be presented in a more systematic, coherent, and elegant way than can be found in the works of the great pioneers. The historical classics in mathematics and science are often written in an outmoded notation. Works of genius as they are, they are also full of false starts, irrelevant bypaths, and blind alleys. The science of our day has already extracted the rich ore and put it in a form which facilitates more rapid comprehension and further progress.

It may be argued, as Spengler does, that mathematics and science are really historical in the sense that they express the cultural values of the age in which they have been developed. According to this view, their meaning and truth-claims are so integrally bound up with the underlying pattern of culture that they cannot be understood in isolation. However this may be with other subjects like art or law, in mathematics and science it is demonstrably false. Whatever is valid in these fields has been incorporated in a continuous and progressive scientific tradition. There may be reasons for approaching the study of mathematics and science historically for certain cultural purposes, but they have nothing to do with the logical necessities of understanding the subject matter.

Aside from the cultural justification for this approach, is there a pedagogical one? Can students acquire greater competence in mathematics and science or a better insight into their character as liberal arts by reading the historical scientific classics than by systematic study? We can do no better than to turn to the mature judgment, based on long years of teaching and active research, of some great mathematicians and scientists.

Our first witness is the distinguished mathematician, Richard Courant, who writes:

> There is no doubt that it is unrealistic to expect a scientific enlightenment of beginners by the study of Euclid, Apollonius, or Ptolemy. It will just give them an oblique perspective of what is important and what is not. Studying the more modern works by Descartes, Newton, etc., except for a few single items, would be even more difficult and likewise not lead to a balanced understanding of mathematics.

Lest Professor Courant be suspected of *parti pris* because he is the author of several texts of high repute, let us hear the judgment of a mathematician whose work is one of the only two books of the twentieth century included on the original St. John's list of great books. Bertrand Russell writes:

> The subject on which you write is one about which I feel very strongly. I think the 'Best Hundred Books' people are utterly absurd on the scientific side. I was myself brought up on Euclid and Newton and I can see the case for them. But on the whole

Euclid is much too slow-moving. Boole is not comparable to his successors. Descartes' geometry is surpassed by every modern textbook of analytical geometry. The broad rule is: historical approach where truth is unattainable, but not in a subject like mathematics or anatomy. (They read Harvey!)

In the field of physical science, none can speak with better qualifications than Albert Einstein:

In my opinion there should be no compulsory reading of classical authors in the field of science. I believe also that the laboratory studies should be selected from a purely pedagogical and not historical point of view. On the other side, I am convinced that lectures concerning the historical development of ideas in different fields are of great value for intelligent students, for such studies are furthering very effectively the independence of judgment and independence from blind belief in temporarily accepted views. I believe that such lectures should be treated as a kind of beautiful luxury and the students should not be bothered with examinations concerning historical facts.

These citations are introduced not as an argument from authority but for the judgments they contain.

The weighty considerations adduced by these witnesses may, of course, be overriden by the empirical findings of controlled experiments in education. Until then it is safe to rely on what they say as expressing both the knowledge and the common sense of the matter.

Eternal and Temporal

There is a kind of hypnotic quality about words like "eternal," "absolute," and "permanent." It prevents many who employ them from designating the specific features within experience to which they refer, and from seeing that because these are worthy of study it does not therefore follow that the "temporal," "relational," and "historical" are unworthy of study. Sometimes failure to see this takes bizarre forms. True liberal education, Mr. Hutchins informs us, concerns itself with *"the abiding and the permanent."* Its first requirement is that it must be intellectual; its second, that it hold up what White-head calls "the habitual vision of greatness"; its third, that "it must deal with permanent and not shifting conditions, with ultimate and not relative ends."[6] Do any of these requirements necessitate that the content of education be constructed primarily around the materials of the past?

That education should be intellectual is indisputable; that it should be only that is highly disputable. The Greek ideal included the education of the intellect as part of the harmonious development of all human faculties. For the Greeks the life of reason was not the reasoning life, any more than the joy of life was a life of joy. The medieval ideal included the education of the intellect as part of the preparation of man for true spirituality. The ideal of *purely* intellectual education, if it has any historical root at all, is an outgrowth of our modern—nay, our contemporary—world of overspecialization. It expresses perhaps what an advanced research scientist might believe the goal of education to be. It is a little ironical that none of the ages glorified in the classical curriculums stressed the ideal of intellectual education or even made it the supreme virtue. This does not thereby invalidate it as an ideal of education. But for present purposes it is enough to point out that no matter how rigorously intellectual education be conceived, there is nothing in the vast collection of *modern* disciplines which prevents them from becoming the medium of such education.

To hold up before students the "habitual vision of greatness" is excellent. But as Whitehead himself emphasizes, this does not mean that the heroes of action and the titans of thought

[6] Hutchins: *Education for Freedom*, p. 57; and second broadcast of the series cited in footnote 5.

inhabit only the realms of the past. Nor does it mean that the study of books, or the study of *great* books, or the study *only* of great books, or the study of great books only of the *past*— to rise in the scale of absurdity—must be central to a liberal education. Great books by all means; but why not also great pictures and symphonies, great plays and cinemas, great social changes and mass movements, as well as the great Armageddons of our own time? We can learn at least as much from the heroic tragedy of Warsaw as from the last stand at Thermopylae. The habitual vision of greatness is important not only because it delights us to lift up our eyes on high but because it gives us working standards of comparative judgment. It enables us to distinguish between the authentic and spurious. It teaches us not to be impatient with what is struggling to be born, to respond to the new and inchoate in the light of its own potentialities of greatness. It helps us to accept the responsibility of making our judgment of greatness here and now, and not timidly playing it safe by deferring to the judgment of the next hundred or thousand years. Absorption in study of the greatness of the past which does not quicken our sense for greatness in the present is a preparation for a life of intellectual snobbery. In face of the emergence of the new, it often leads to a kind of cultural philistinism. "To have spent one's youth at college," writes William James, "in contact with the choice and rare and precious, and yet still to be a blind prig or vulgarian, unable to scent out human excellence or to divine it amid its accidents, to know it only when ticketed and labelled and forced on us by others, this indeed should be accounted the very calamity and shipwreck of a higher education."[7]

Even more grandiose is Mr. Hutchins's demand that liberal education deal "with permanent and not shifting conditions, with ultimate and not relative ends." But not very sensible!

[7] William James: "Value of the College Bred," reprinted in *Essays for College Men* (ed. Norman Foerster, Frederick A. Manchester, and Karl Young; New York: D. C. Heath & Co.; 1913), p. 167.

Slavery, feudalism, capitalism, the rise and decline of great empires, colonial and revolutionary America, the migrations of peoples, and the patterns of technological change—all would have to be excluded from a liberal education. For they certainly are not permanent. Indeed, everything historical would evaporate from the course of study. But if so, then why study *Greek* culture? And if Greek culture, why not American? And if there is something permanent in historical change, why is it privileged over what is not permanent? How can we distinguish which is which, without studying *both*? The same argument applies to "ultimate" and "relative" ends. This is a distinction in a certain theory of value. But values as given are not labelled "ultimate" or "relative." Under either label they may be equally valid in their respective contexts. Is it true, as a matter of fact or analysis, that what are called "ultimate" values have the same meaning, as distinct from their formal verbal expression, in all times, places, and cultures? How can we tell without examining the values of at least some *different* cultures? But this is an argument for comparative culture study and critical anthropology which, though it tames the fanaticism of virtue, need not lead, as Mr. Hutchins fears, to the identification of custom and morality.

Grant for the moment all of Mr. Hutchins' dubious premises. Grant that there are eternal problems and eternal truths. Why cannot they emerge from a consideration of the important issues of *our* age? *What is eternally true must be true at any time, including the present.* The half-unconscious identification of the eternal with the ancient, of the permanent with the past, has continuously been drawn in history. It is not for nothing that governments are always on the side of the eternal. But metaphysical and political issues aside, a program like the one Mr. Hutchins advocates is educationally unsound. For whatever the alleged advantages of a curriculum organized around the materials of the past—and all curriculums have some advantages—they can also be won by an intelligent analysis of modern culture. The enormous differential gain in the modern approach is that the knowledge and values which emerge from inquiries into the massive and dramatic problems of our times have a definite relevance to the perennial task of making life better here and now. On the other hand, if we assume that we already are in possession of eternal truths that need only be applied to the present, we are likely to overlook what is distinctive in our own times. There is a natural bias to discount the evidence showing that propositions believed eternally true are actually false or have only *a limited historical validity*. The creative sterility of modern adherents of great systems of past thought is in part due to their failure to dip into the fresh seas of contemporary experience in order to test and amplify their stock of "eternal truths."

The whole notion that the past is to be ransacked only to discover the "truths" it can bequeath to the present is parochial. Its more fruitful use, as in literature and art, where the past is not directly relevant to present-day social problems or programs of action, is the ever-present occasion it offers for the enlargement of meanings and the cultivation of the imagination.

Tradition

It is often alleged that a modern curriculum sins against tradition, and thus violates one of the deepest hungers of man, continuity with the past. But as important as tradition is, reflection makes clear that by itself it cannot determine the content of instruction. No matter what turning in the road we take, it is continuous with the road by which we have come. And there are few things we can do today for which some warrant in past traditions cannot be found. Those who defend tradition in education would be the first to deny that the traditional is synonymous with the dead or obsolete. How, then, do we distinguish between obsolete and living traditions? When traditions are invoked to settle issues, they are always *selections* from the heritage of the past—judgments of comparative worth or value testifying to needs in the present—and are justified by their consequences.

The deepest traditions of a community are those that are so completely taken for granted that they rarely emerge on the level of critical awareness, and still more rarely become subjects of debate—like our language and folkways. But let an issue once force itself on the attention of a community to the point of arousing discussion; then it becomes obvious that what the tradition *has been*, of itself does not decide. It is we who decide what our tradition *should be*. The past is so rich that we can always find an historical paternity to legitimize our current offspring.

Those who appeal to tradition as a bulwark against change are curiously unaware of its actual content. For most traditions represent departures from earlier traditions, and their subsequent history is full of further departures from their original purposes and beginnings. No one can survey the history of American religious practice, for example, without realizing that tolerance to dissenters marked a break with earlier traditions, and that the recognition of equal rights for all religions marked a departure from the tradition of mere tolerance. How much truer is this for the history of Western culture. Those who speak of *the* great tradition of the Western world, and charge "decadent" liberals with attempting to ignore it, betray an insensitiveness to the richness, complexity, and contradictory features of what is summed up by the phrase. The dominant traditions of Greek culture are at least as fundamentally different from those of medieval Christendom as the latter are from the traditions of the Renaissance, the Reformation, and the American, the French, and the Industrial Revolutions. In different respects, we are the inheritors of them all. Our indiscriminate allegiance to them testifies to a basic confusion in our purposes and values. It is an evasion of the challenge of our own time and culture.

The function of a liberal education in the modern world is to bring some degree of order to minds that have inherited conflicting traditions. It must weave the problems and materials of the modern world into a recognizable pattern by which individuals may take their bearings for a full and responsible life. In liberating individuals from confusion, such education liberates within them fresh energies to redirect or remake, separately and together, the worlds they live in. If their action is enlightened, it will increase human freedom by extending control of nature; if it is mature, it will enhance the quality of freedom by bringing the control of nature under wise human control.

Subject Matters and Skills

What, concretely, should the modern man know in order to live intelligently in the world today? What should we require that he learn of subject matters and skills in his educational career in order that he may acquire maturity in feeling, in judgment, in action? Can we indicate the minimum indispensables of a liberal education in the modern world? This approach recognizes that no subject per se is inherently liberal at all times and places. But it also recognizes that within a given age in a given culture, the enlightenment and maturity, the freedom and power, which liberal education aims to impart, is more likely to be achieved by mastery of some subject matters and skills than by others. In short, principles must bear fruit in specific programs in specific times. In what follows I shall speak of studies rather than of conventional courses.

(1) The liberally educated person should be intellectually at home in the world of physical nature. He should know something about the earth he inhabits and its place in the solar

system, about the solar system and its relation to the cosmos. He should know something about mechanics, heat, light, electricity, and magnetism as the universal forces that condition anything he is or may become. He should be just as intimately acquainted with the nature of man as a biological species, his evolution, and the discoveries of experimental genetics. He should know something about the structure of his own body and mind, and the cycle of birth, growth, learning, and decline. To have even a glimmer of understanding of these things, he must go beyond the level of primary description and acquire some grasp of the principles that explain what he observes. Where an intelligent grasp of principles requires a knowledge of mathematics, its fundamental ideas should be presented in such a way that students carry away the sense of mathematics not only as a tool for the solution of problems but as a study of types of order, system, and language.

Such knowledge is important to the individual *not* merely because of its intrinsic fascination. Every subject from numismatics to Sanskrit possesses an intrinsic interest to those who are curious about it. It is important because it helps make everyday experience more intelligible; because it furnishes a continuous exemplification of scientific method in action; because our world is literally being remade by the consequences and applications of science; because the fate of nations and the vocations of men depend upon the use of this knowledge; and because it provides the instruments to reduce our vast helplessness and dependence in an uncertain world.

Such knowledge is no less important because it bears upon the formation of *rational belief* about the place of man in the universe. Whatever views a man professes today about God, human freedom, Cosmic Purpose, and personal survival, he cannot reasonably hold them in ignorance of the scientific account of the world and man.

These are some of the reasons why the study of the natural sciences, and the elementary mathematical notions they involve, should be *required* of everyone. Making such study required imposes a heavy obligation and a difficult task of pedagogical discovery upon those who teach it. It is commonly recognized that the sciences today are taught as if all students enrolled in science courses were preparing to be professional scientists. Most of them are not. Naturally they seek to escape a study whose wider and larger uses they do not see because many of their teachers do not see it. Here is not the place to canvass and evaluate the attempts being made to organize instruction in the sciences. The best experience seems to show that one science should not be taken as the exemplar of all, but that the basic subject matter of astronomy, physics, chemistry, geology, in one group, and biology and psychology in another, should be covered. For when only one science is taught it tends to be treated professionally. Similarly, the best experience indicates that instruction should be interdepartmental—any competent teacher from one of these fields in either group should be able to teach all of them in the group, instead of having a succession of different teachers each representing his own field. This usually destroys both the continuity and the cumulative effect of the teaching as a whole.

(2) Every student should be required to become intelligently aware of how the society in which he lives functions, of the great forces molding contemporary civilization, and of the crucial problems of our age which await decision. The studies most appropriate to this awareness have been conventionally separated into history, economics, government, sociology, social psychology, and anthropology. This separation is an intellectual scandal. For it is impossible to have an adequate grasp of the problems of government without a knowledge of economics, and vice versa. Except for some special domains of professional interest, the same is true for the other subjects as well.

The place of the social studies, properly integrated around

problems and issues, is fundamental in the curriculum of modern education. It is one of the dividing points between the major conflicting schools of educational thought. The question of its justification must be sharply distinguished from discussion of the relative merits of this or that mode of approach to the social studies.

The knowledge and insight that the social studies can give are necessary for every student because no matter what his specialized pursuits may later be, the extent to which he can follow them, and the "contextual" developments within these fields, depend upon the total social situation of which they are in some sense a part. An engineer today whose knowledge is restricted only to technical matters of engineering, or a physician whose competence extends only to the subject matter of traditional medical training, is ill-prepared to plan intelligently for a life-career or to understand the basic problems that face his profession. He is often unable to cope adequately with those specific problems in his own domain that involve, as so many problems of social and personal health do, economic and psychological difficulties. No matter what an individual's vocation, the conditions of his effective functioning depend upon pervasive social tendencies which set the occasions for the application of knowledge, provide the opportunities of employment, and not seldom determine even the direction of research.

More important, the whole presupposition of the theory of democracy is that the electorate will be able to make intelligent decisions on the issues before it. These issues are basically political, social, and economic. Their specific character changes from year to year. But their generic form, and the character of the basic problems, do not. Nor, most essential of all, do the proper intellectual habits of meeting them change. It is undeniably true that the world we live in is one marked by greater changes, because of the impact of technology, than ever before. This does not necessitate changing the curriculum daily to catch up with today's newspapers, nor does it justify a concentration on presumably eternal problems as if these problems had significance independent of cultural place-time. The fact that we are living in a world where the rate of cultural change is greater than at any time in the past, together with its ramifications, may itself become a central consideration for analysis.

The construction of a social studies curriculum is a task of the greatest difficulty even after the artificiality of departmental lines of division has been recognized. For the integration of the material demands a historical approach, set not by bare chronology, but by the problems themselves. It must incorporate large amounts of philosophy and the scientific disciplines of evaluating judgments of fact and value. It must abandon misconceived interpretations of the "institutional approach" which describe social practices without confronting the challenge of theories and problems. It must not shrink from considering "solutions," and at the same time must guard against indoctrination of conclusions. It must learn how to use our life in cities, factories, and fields as a kind of "laboratory," not as occasions for sight-seeing excursions of dubious educational significance.

Properly organized studies of this kind are not something which already exist. They are something to be achieved. Their content must be definite and yet not fixed in detail. They do not exclude treatment of historical background but relate it to something of momentous issue in the present. They do not exclude great books of the past and present, nor bad books, nor material not found in books.

One of the reasons for the low estate in which the social studies are held is the failure to recognize the distinction between the general pattern of inquiry, whose logic holds for all fields in which truth is sought, and the specific criteria of validity, which are appropriate to special domains. We are all familiar with the type of historian who thinks "geometrically," i.e., who believes he can reach conclusions about human beings in historical situations with almost the same degree of rigor he uses to reach conclusions about triangles and circles. The warning against taking certain standards of precision as a model for all fields is at least as old as Aristotle.

Discussion," he says, "will be adequate if it has as much clearness as the subject-matter admits of, for precision is not to be sought for alike in all discussions . . . it is the mark of an educated man to look for precision in each class of things just so far as the nature of the subject admits; it is evidently equally foolish to accept prob-able reasoning from a mathematician and to demand from a rhetorician scientific proofs.[8]

Nonetheless, most discussions of the content of a liberal education which are heavily accented with a bias towards classic studies sin against this wisdom. In such accounts, mathe-matics and physics are justified as models of precise thought on which the social sciences are to pattern themselves. It is overlooked that the "logic" of mathematics and physics is a specific application of the general pattern of inquiry. Its pre-cision reflects the nature of the subject matter considered. A physician, an economist, an anthropologist—even a biologist—who sought to carry into his domain the same standards would get grotesque results. *The models of correct thinking in each field must be the best illustrations of thinking in that field, not the pattern of another field.* "The type of exercise in con-sistent thinking" in mathematics is one thing, in the field of psychosomatic medicine it is quite another; "fidelity to em-pirical data" in astronomy is something else again from "fidelity to empirical data" in linguistics. This is blurred over in passages like the following from books on liberal education which, even when they give the social studies a place in the liberal arts curriculum, do so in a grudging and suspicious way:

[8] Aristotle: *Nicomachean Ethics* (tr. Ross; Oxford: Oxford University Press; 1942), 1094b 12–14, 24–27.

. . . The social studies cannot compete with pure mathematics and the natural sciences in exhaustive analysis, rigorous inference, or verifiable interpretations. Their methods are by nature such as to forbid the substitution of these studies for the more precise and established disciplines. The latter must continue to supply a distinctive and fundamental type of exercise in consistent reasoning and fidelity to empirical data.[9]

Literally read, this may seem to provide for the independence of social studies: but it is obvious from its overtones that an invidious distinction is being drawn between the mathematical-physical sciences on the one hand, and the social sciences on the other.

(3) Everyone recognizes a distinction between knowledge and wisdom. This distinction is not clarified by making a mystery of wisdom and speaking of it as if it were begotten by divine inspiration while knowledge had a more lowly source. Wisdom is a kind of knowledge. It is knowledge of the nature, career, and consequences of *human values*. Since these cannot be separated from the human organism and the social scene, the moral ways of man cannot be understood without knowledge of the ways of things and institutions.

To study social affairs without an analysis of policies is to lose oneself in factual minutiae that lack interest and relevance. But knowledge of values is a prerequisite of the intelligent determination of policy. Philosophy, most broadly viewed, is the critical survey of existence from the standpoint of value. This points to the twofold role of philosophy in the curriculum of the college.

The world of physical nature may be studied without reference to human values. But history, art, literature, and particularly the social studies involve problems of value at every

[9] Greene, *et al.*: *Liberal Education Re-Examined*, pp. 56–7.

turn. A social philosophy whose implications are worked out
is a series of proposals that something be *done* in the world.
It includes a set of *plans* to conserve or change aspects of
social life. Today the community is arrayed under different
banners without a clear understanding of the basic issues involved. In the press of controversy, the ideals and values at the
heart of every social philosophy are widely affirmed as articles
of blind faith. They are partisan commitments justified only
by the emotional security they give to believers. They spread
by contagion, unchecked by critical safeguards; yet the future
of civilization largely depends upon them and how they are
held. It is therefore requisite that their study be made an
integral part of the liberal arts curriculum. Systematic and
critical instruction should be given in the great maps of life—
the ways to heaven, hell, and earth—which are being unrolled
in the world today.

Ideals and philosophies of life are not parts of the world of
nature; but it is a pernicious illusion to imagine that they cannot be studied "scientifically." Their historical origins, their
concatenation of doctrine, their controlling assumptions, their
means, methods, and consequences in practice, can and should
be investigated in a scientific spirit. There are certain social
philosophies that would forbid such an investigation for fear
of not being able to survive it; but it is one of the great merits
of the democratic way of life and one of its strongest claims
for acceptance that it can withstand analysis of this sort. It is
incumbent upon the liberal arts college to provide for close
study of the dominant social and political philosophies, ranging from one end of the color-spectrum to the other. Proper
study will disclose that these philosophies cannot be narrowly
considered in their own terms. They involve an examination
of the great ways of life—of the great visions of philosophy
which come into play whenever we try to arrange our values
in a preference scale in order to choose the better between
conflicting goods. Philosophy is best taught when the issues

of moral choice arise naturally out of the problems of social
life. The effective integration of concrete materials from history, literature, and social studies can easily be achieved within
a philosophical perspective.

(4) Instruction in the natural, social, and technological forces
shaping the world, and in the dominant conflicting ideals in
behalf of which these forces are to be controlled, goes a long
way. But not far enough. Far more important than knowledge
is the method by which it is reached, and the ability to recognize when it constitutes *evidence* and when not; and more
important than any particular ideal is the way in which it is
held, and the capacity to evaluate it in relation to other ideals.
From first to last, in season and out, our educational institutions, especially on the college level, must emphasize *methods*
of analysis. They must build up in students a critical sense of
evidence, relevance, and validity against which the multi-
tudinous seas of propaganda will wash in vain. They must
strengthen the powers of independent reflection, which will
enable students to confront the claims of ideals and values by
their alternatives and the relative costs of achieving them.

The objections to this stress on method come from the most
diverse quarters and are based on the crassest misunderstanding of the nature of methodological analysis and the reasons
for making it central, not exclusive, in every educational enterprise. These objections we shall consider in a special chapter.
We shall first indicate the way in which this emphasis on
method is to be incorporated in the curriculum.

It is taken for granted that every subject taught will be
taught in a fashion that will bring home the ways in which
warranted conclusions are reached. But it is well known that
the habits of correct thinking are not carried over from one
field to another unless the second field is similar in nature to
the first. We do not need to wait for the results of experiments

on transference of training to realize that a great many able scientists who pontificate on matters outside their fields display not only ignorance but utter inability to grasp essential points at issue or to make valid elementary inferences. More and more, thinking is becoming thinking in specialized domains, largely professional, accompanied by the feeling that outside that domain it is unimportant what conclusions are reached, or by the feeling that any conclusion is as valid as any other.

Those who believe that this state of affairs can be rectified by giving a course in some special subject matter like mathematics or Latin have never confronted the challenge to provide evidence for their claim. To teach something else in order to teach *how to think* is not a short cut to logic but a circuitous way to nowhere.

There are some who deny that there is a power of general thought, that thinking is a habit that always has a specific locus in a definite field, and that there is no carry-over from one field to a widely dissimilar one. In a certain sense, this is true. But we certainly can distinguish between domains or fields of interest which are broad and those that are narrow; and between those domains in which everyone has an interest because it affects him as a human being and citizen, and those domains that are more specialized.

The field of language, of inference and argument, is a broad field but a definite one in which specific training can be given to all students. How to read intelligently, how to recognize good from bad reasoning, how to evaluate evidence, how to distinguish between a definition and a hypothesis and between a hypothesis and a resolution, can be taught in such a way as to build up permanent habits of logic in action. The result of thorough training in "semantic" analysis—using that term in its broadest sense without invidious distinctions between different schools—is an intellectual sophistication without which a man may be learned but not intelligent.

Judging by past and present curricular achievements in developing students with intellectual sophistication and maturity, our colleges must be pronounced in the main, dismal failures. The main reason for the failure is the absence of serious effort, except in a few institutions, to realize this goal. The necessity of the task is not even recognized. This failure is not only intellectually reprehensible; it is socially dangerous. For the natural susceptibility of youth to enthusiasms, its tendency to glorify action, and its limited experience make it easy recruiting material for all sorts of demagogic movements which flatter its strength and impatience. Recent history furnishes many illustrations of how, in the absence of strong critical sense, youthful strength can lead to cruelty, and youthful impatience to folly. It is true that people who are incapable of thinking cannot be taught how to think, and that the incapacity for thought is not restricted to those who learn. But the first cannot be judged without being exposed to the processes of critical instruction, and the second should be eliminated from the ranks of the teachers. There is considerable evidence to show that students who are capable of completing high school can be so taught that they are aware of *whether* they are thinking or not. There is hope that, with better pedagogic skill and inspiration, they may become capable of grasping the main thought of *what* they are reading or hearing in non-technical fields—of developing a sense of *what validly follows from what,* an accompanying sensitiveness to the dominant types of fallacies, and a habit of weighing evidence for conclusions advanced.

My own experience has led me to the conclusion that this is *not* accomplished by courses in formal logic which, when given in a rigorous and elegant way, accomplish little more than courses in pure mathematics. There is an approach to the study of logic that on an elementary level is much more successful in achieving the ends described above than the traditional course in formal logic. This plunges the student into an analysis of language material around him. By constant use of concrete illustrations drawn from all fields, but especially the fields of politics and social study, insight is developed into the logical principles of definition, the structure of analogies, dilemmas, types of fallacies and the reasons *why* they are fallacies, the criteria of good hypotheses, and related topics. Such training may legitimately be required of all students. Although philosophers are usually best able to give it, any teacher who combines logical capacity with pedagogic skill can make this study a stimulating experience.

(5) There is less controversy about the desirability of the study of composition and literature than about any other subject in the traditional or modern curriculum. It is appreciated that among the essentials of clear thought are good language habits and that, except in the higher strata of philosophic discourse, tortuous obscurities of expression are more likely to be an indication of plain confusion than of stuttering profundity. It is also widely recognized that nothing can take the place of literature in developing the imagination, and in imparting a sense of the inexhaustible richness of human personality. The questions that arise at this point are not of justification, but of method, technique, and scope of comprehensiveness.

If good language habits are to be acquired *only* in order to acquire facility in thinking, little can be said for the conventional courses in English composition. Students cannot acquire facility in clear expression in the space of a year, by developing sundry themes from varied sources, under the tutelage of instructors whose training and interest may not qualify them for sustained critical thought. Clear thinking is best controlled by those who are at home in the field in which thinking is done. If language instruction is to be motivated only by the desire to strengthen the power of organizing ideas in written discourse, it should be left to properly trained instructors in other disciplines.

But there are other justifications for teaching students English composition. The first is that there are certain rules of intelligent reading that are essential to—if they do not constitute—understanding. These rules are very elementary. By themselves they do not tell us how to understand a poem, a mathematical demonstration, a scientific text, or a religious prayer—all of which require special skills. But they make it easier for the student to uncover the nature of the "argument" —what is being said, what is being assumed, what is being presented as evidence—in any piece of prose that is not a narrative or simply informational in content. In a sense these rules are integral to the study of logic in action, but in such an introductory way that they are usually not considered part of logical study which begins its work after basic meanings have been established, or in independence of the meaning of logical symbols.

Another reason for teaching English composition independently is its uses in learning how to write. "Effective writing" is not necessarily the same thing as logical writing. The purpose for which we write determines whether our writing is effective. And there are many situations in which we write not to convince or to prove but to explain, arouse, confess, challenge, or assuage. To write *interestingly* may sometimes be just as important as to write soundly because getting a hearing and keeping attention may depend upon it. How much of the skills of writing can be taught is difficult to say. That it is worth making the effort to teach these skills is indisputable.

The place of language in the curriculum involves not merely our native language but *foreign* languages. Vocational considerations aside, should knowledge of a foreign language be required, and why?

Here again the discussion reveals great confusion. Most of the reasons advanced for making knowledge of a foreign language required are either demonstrably false or question-begging. There is a valid reason for making such study prescribed, but it is rarely stated.

It is sometimes asserted that no one can understand the structure of his own language unless he understands the structure of another. By "structure" is usually meant the grammar of the language.

> The study of Greek and Latin has a special value in increasing an American student's understanding of his own language. . . . The study of Greek and Latin provides one of the best introductions to the role of inflection in our grammatical methods and, by contrast, to an understanding of the function of other devices we now use in place of inflections.[1]

> . . . One's own language should be known as well as possible in terms of its peculiar genius; and at least one other language—Greek is still the best one for the purpose, and indeed for any purpose [*sic!*]—should be equally known. The lines of any two languages converge in the structure of language itself.[2]

The assumption behind these passages is that mastery of the intricacies of English grammar makes for greater ability in writing, reading, and understanding modern English prose. No evidence has ever been offered for this statement and many intelligent teachers of English deny it. The best grammarians are conspicuously not the best speakers and writers of English. It is one thing to have grammar "in the bones" as a consequence of acquiring good habits of speech and writing. It is quite another to learn grammar as a means of acquiring those habits. There are better and more direct ways to that goal. But let us grant the questionable assumption. The recommendations in the quoted passages would still be a horrendous *non sequitur*. For there is every reason to believe that if the time

[1] Ibid., p. 58.
[2] Mark van Doren: *Liberal Education* (New York: Henry Holt & Company; 1943), pp. 131-2.

spent on learning the grammar of foreign languages were devoted to more intensive and prolonged study of English, the result would be far greater proficiency in English than if the available time were divided between the two languages.

A second reason often advanced for making the study of foreign languages mandatory, especially Greek and Latin, is that it contributes to the enrichment of the English vocabulary of students, and gives them a sense for shades of meaning in use which is necessary for even a fair degree of mastery of our language. The following is representative of claims of this character:

> Although many of these words have now certain semantic values that were foreign to their use in their original settings, still an experience of these words in contexts of Greek and Latin provides an insight into their functioning in English *which no other experience can give.*[3]

What a breath-taking piece of dogmatism! All the evidence is begged. Once more, the obvious advantage of devoting the time spent on foreign language to additional study of English words in use is evaded. It is further assumed that Greek and Latin must be systematically studied in order to learn the historical derivation of the English words we owe these languages. Courses have been devised in which Greek and Latin words in current English use are studied without intensive study of these languages. It is still an open question whether an intensive study of the English language helps students understand the meanings of the words they encounter in the study of Greek and Latin rather than vice versa. It has often been observed that in sight reading of Greek and Latin, when students cannot consult dictionaries, those who are already most proficient in English do much better than those whose English vocabularies are limited.

[3] Greene, *et. al.*: *Liberal Education Re-Examined*, p. 59. My italics.

The main reason why students should be requested to learn another language is that it is the most effective medium by which, when properly taught, they can acquire a sensitivity to language, to the subtle tones, undertones, and overtones of words, and to the licit ambiguities of imaginative discourse. No one who has not translated prose or poetry from one language to another can appreciate both the unique richness and the unique limitations of his own language. This is particularly true where the life of the emotions is concerned; and it is particularly important that it should be realized. For the appreciation of emotions, perhaps even their recognition in certain cases, depends upon their linguistic identification. The spectrum of human emotions is much more dense than the words by which we render them. Knowledge of different languages, and the attempts made to communicate back and forth between them in our own minds, broaden and diversify our own feelings. They multiply points of view, and liberate us from the prejudice that words—*our* words—are the natural signs of things and events. The genius of a culture is exemplified in a pre-eminent way in the characteristic idioms of its language. In learning another language we enable ourselves to appreciate both the cultural similarities and differences of the Western world.

So far as I know, this argument for the teaching of foreign languages was first advanced by Warner Fite.[4] But it is allied with a disparagement of "abstract thinking" on the ground that, since symbolic or conceptual thought strives to dissociate itself from the particularities of images and qualities, in the nature of the case it must falsify the fluidities of experience. This is a very serious error. Two things do not have to be identical in order to be characterized by identical relationships. And it is the relationships between things which are expressed in the symbols of abstract thinking. There is no opposition

[4] Warner Fite: "The Philosopher and His Words," *Philosophical Review*, Vol. 44, No. 2 (March 1935), p. 120.

between "abstract thinking" and "concrete" or "qualitative" thinking. They involve differences in emphasis, subject matter, and interest, not different logics or formal criteria of validity.

The place of literature in the curriculum is justified by so many considerations that it is secure against all criticism. Here, too, what is at issue is not whether literature—Greek, Latin, English, European, American—should be read and studied in the schools but what should be read, when, and by what methods. These are details, important details—but outside the scope of our inquiry.

Something should be said about the unique opportunity which the teaching of literature provides, not only in giving delight by heightening perception of the formal values of literary craftsmanship, but in giving insight into people. The opposite of a liberal education, William James somewhere suggests, is a literal education. A literal education is one which equips a person to read formulas and equations, straightforward prose, doggerel verse, and advertising signs. It does not equip one to read the language of metaphor, of paradox, of indirect analogy, of serious fancy in which the emotions and passions and half-believed ideas of human beings express themselves. To read great literature is to read men—their fears and motives, their needs and hopes. Every great novelist is a *Menschenkenner* who opens the hearts of others to us and helps us to read our own hearts as well. The intelligent study of literature should never directly aim to strengthen morals and improve manners. For its natural consequences are a delicacy of perception and an emotional tact that are defeated by preaching and didactic teaching.

A liberal education will impart an awareness of the amazing and precious complexity of human relationships. Since those relationships are violated more often out of insensitiveness than out of deliberate intent, whatever increases sensitiveness of perception and understanding humanizes life. Literature in all its forms is the great humanizing medium of life. It must therefore be representative of life; not only of past life but of our own; not only of our own culture but of different cultures.

(6) An unfailing mark of philistinism in education is reference to the study of art and music as "the frills and fads" of schooling. Insofar as those who speak this way are not tone-deaf or color-blind, they are themselves products of a narrow education, unaware of the profound experiences which are uniquely bound up with the trained perception of color and form. There is no reason to believe that the capacity for the appreciation of art and music shows a markedly different curve of distribution from what is observable in the measurement of capacity of drawing inferences or recalling relevant information. A sufficient justification for making some study of art and music required in modern education is that it provides an unfailing source of delight in personal experience, a certain grace in living, and a variety of dimensions of meaning by which to interpret the world around us. This is a sufficient justification: there are others, quite subsidiary, related to the themes, the occasions, the history and backgrounds of the works studied. Perhaps one should add—although this expresses only a reasonable hope—that a community whose citizens have developed tastes would not tolerate the stridency, the ugliness and squalor which assault us in our factories, our cities, and our countryside.

One of the reasons why the study of art and music has not received as much attention as it should by educators, particularly on the college level, is that instruction in these subjects often suffers from two opposite defects. Sometimes courses in art and music are given as if all students enrolled in them were planning a career as practicing artists or as professional *teachers* of the arts. Sometimes they are given as hours for passive enjoyment or relaxation in which the teacher does the performing or talking and in which there is no call upon the students to make an intelligent response.

The key-stress in courses in art and music should be *discrimination* and *interpretation*, rather than appreciation and cultivation. The latter can take care of themselves, when the student has learned to discriminate and interpret intelligently.

Briefly summarized: the answer to the question *What should we teach?* is selected materials from the fields of mathematics and the natural sciences; social studies, including history; language and literature; philosophy and logic; art and music. The knowledge imparted by such study should be acquired in such a way as to strengthen the skills of reading and writing, of thinking and imaginative interpretation, of criticism and evaluation.

The content of education as here described finds its most direct application on the college level. It indicates the knowledge, the values, the habits of thought and feeling which educators must have before them as objectives in constructing and revising curriculums, and in guiding and teaching students.

The same principles apply, *mutatis mutandis*, to education on the lower levels. Those who are not professional educators may feel that this is shockingly "high-brow" and unrealistic. But once due allowance is made for the difference in powers of children at various ages in the preparation of teaching materials, in themes for emphasis, and specific techniques of instruction, the air of paradox and unrealism disappears. It is not necessary to discuss with children in the fourth or fifth grade "the evils of capitalism"—a typical illustration employed by those who caricature the philosophy of progressive education; at that level, social studies can begin with problems that are always found whenever children work or study or play in groups. It cannot be expected that the only conclusions presented to children will be ones for which they can see the logical or empirical reasons. Otherwise, they will never learn that twice two is four, or that honesty is desirable even when it isn't the best immediate policy. But the school cannot begin at too early an age to strengthen the child's powers of intelligence and to develop habits of reasonableness, even if on some crucial matters it must supplement them with other methods of suasion until he reaches maturity and can rationally test these matters for himself. The teacher may have to step in to stop a child from undertaking an experiment from which the child, or those on whom he practices it, may not recover. The direction, however, that teaching should take is such as to progressively reduce the frequency of authoritative intrusion into the learning process. This brings us to a set of questions that bear more directly on the methods of teaching. Before turning to them we must consider a problem set by what has been excluded from this outline of a required minimum of studies in a liberal education.

Religion

There is one course of study whose absence from the minimum indispensables of a liberal education we would not have needed to justify a generation ago. But, because of a widely organized campaign for its introduction into public schools and colleges, something must be said of it. This is the study of religion and theology. In the curriculum I have described, ideas and events and leading figures associated with great religious movements are naturally, indeed inescapably, a part of studies dealing with literary, social, historical, and philosophical subject matter. Our modern world is incomprehensible without them, particularly the Reformation. And no bar exists that would prevent an interested student from continuing his education in religion and theology after, or even while, devoting himself to the required curriculum—either in or outside school. Obviously, then, the demand for the introduction of required religious and theological study is not motivated merely by the desire for the cultural enrichment of the curriculum. The Bible, for example, is to be studied not as great literature but as revealed, religious truth.[5]

Nor can the compulsory study of these subjects be justified by the worthy desire to elevate character and improve moral behavior. For anyone who has lived with intelligent and growing minds will have discovered that there is hardly anything they resent so much as didactic moralizing, even when it has the weight of authority—natural or supernatural—behind it. Virtues are primarily matters of habit. The schools can never succeed in teaching the decencies of behavior where the home, the neighborhood, the church have failed. At best, the school can have an indirect moral effect by developing within students imaginative sympathy for others' feelings and needs, awareness of how our destinies are interrelated by common predicaments, and a thoughtfulness about the consequences of our actions on the delicate web of human relationships.

Is the study of religion and theology prerequisite to the achievement of these qualities? Have they a monopoly on the discovery and effective teaching of moral ideals? The history of moral insight from Socrates to Dewey, from Epicurus to Santayana, refutes the claim. Neither the meaning nor the validity of moral ideals rests on supernatural foundations. More, there is no evidence, Napoleon and Metternich to the contrary notwithstanding, that even *belief* in the existence of the supernatural is an essential condition for public order or private morality. Among those who are moved by fear, fear of the Lord is not as potent as fear of the Law in inhibiting immoral impulses. And both—besides being very ignoble

[5] For an excellent study of this question, particularly on the use of the Bible in the classroom, cf. Conrad H. Moehlman: *School and Church: The American Way* (New York: Harper & Brothers; 1944). Dr. Moehlman was, until his death in 1961, Professor of the History of Christianity at the Colgate-Rochester Divinity School.

grounds for living a good life—are far weaker than the habits acquired before the meanings of these abstract ideas are understood. Whoever holds the opinion that religious education is either a necessary or a sufficient condition for the prevention of crime, does so in defiance of available statistics on the subject.

Whatever other reasons are advanced for making the study of religion and theology part of the minimum indispensables of a liberal education, the chief reason is that they allegedly teach important *truths* about the world, man, and God which no other discipline is competent to judge; that these truths are the copestones of the whole structure of knowledge, whether of fact or value; and that, deprived of them, education as well as life is radically defective, without center, balance, or proper subordination of part to part.

If these claims were true, no reasonable person could object to the inclusion of religious studies in a liberal education. It should be borne in mind, however, that no course in philosophy can be complete without some critical evaluation, not of the dogmas of any specific theology, but of the generic *type* of claims made, leaving open to the student the choice and adjustment of his religious beliefs in the light of philosophical discussion. Similarly, in the study of geology or biology a critical evaluation of the evidence for the theory of evolution is made without considering specific theological dogmas about Genesis. But a *critical* evaluation of dogmas is precisely what those who urge the prescription of religious and theological study do *not* want. Imagine what an outcry would arise from religious organizations if their sacred dogmas were critically evaluated—and possibly rejected. Religious dogmas can be imparted only by those who have faith to others of the same faith. The function of what is called reason in this connection is only to clear the ground of obstacles to ultimate acceptance of a truth already known. Those who teach these subjects teach to be believed, not to provoke doubts or questions or initiate fresh inquiries. By their own admission they propose to offer, literally, courses in apologetics.

To introduce these studies is therefore to make a sharp break with the critical methods of inquiry followed in other disciplines of the curriculum. Worse, since no revealed truth admits the supremacy of any method by which its deliverances are to be tested, to prescribe these studies in a community of many different faiths and revealed truths is to revive the insoluble religious controversies of the past with all their dangers. To divide students according to their faiths, as M. Maritain suggests in an effort to obviate these dangers,[6] and to turn them over to theologians of different denominations for instruction in the mysteries of salvation and damnation, is to undermine that fellowship of intelligence and learning which defines a genuine liberal arts college.

When it is recalled that the community places no restriction on the voluntary study of religion and theology under denominational auspices, the demand for required instruction in them rightly becomes suspicious. It suggests a fear that religious dogmas may lose out in the free competition of ideas in a democratic culture and a desire to safeguard those who have the true faith from the crises born of intellectual growth. It suggests a plan to use the schools in order to reach those who cannot be drawn, by their own inner compulsion or by the promise of eternity, to ecclesiastical authority. It is an expression of "the new failure of nerve" and a step to end the separation of church and state in America.

Those who use the term "religious" without any supernatural or doctrinal connotations, like John Dewey and Alfred North Whitehead in some of their writings, do not call for the introduction of religion as a specific subject of instruction in the

[6] Jacques Maritain: *Education at the Crossroads* (New Haven: Yale University Press; 1943), p. 75.

curriculum. To them a truly religious education has an entirely different meaning. It is found wherever knowledge is so taught that it heightens the sense of human responsibility for the inescapable decisions which men must make. "Religious" here is synonymous with "moral" in its broadest sense. It is a pervasive feeling and attitude nurtured by the whole educational enterprise when, freed from superstition, it devotes itself to truth in the service of man. It is a form of natural piety not merely towards existence but to the ideal possibilities of a better existence.

This conception of religious education is so utterly different from what is customarily called "religious education" that it seems wiser to use a phrase with fewer conventional overtones. But its meaning is clear enough. "A religious education," says Whitehead, "is an education which inculcates duty and reverence. Duty arises from our potential control over the course of events. Where attainable knowledge could have changed the issue, ignorance has the guilt of vice. And the foundation of reverence is this perception, that the present holds within itself the complete sum of existence, backwards and forwards, that whole amplitude of time, which is eternity."[7]

[7] Alfred North Whitehead: *The Aims of Education and Other Essays* (New York: The Macmillan Company; 1929), p. 23.

Chapter 7

THE CENTRALITY OF
METHOD

"The science and art of democratic education treats it as a continuing process from birth to death, subordinates transmitting the past to creating a future different from the past, makes precept a function of practice, exalts variation over repetition and encourages the free co-operation of differences to displace the regimented reproduction of identicals, prefers the doubt, the enquiry, the experiment of competitive co-operation and co-operative competition of the sciences to the obedient credulity and unquestioning rehearsals of dogmatic faiths."

HORACE M. KALLEN

FROM THE point of view of content, the focal problems of our age cannot be isolated in one compartment of studies. All studies of the required area, in varying degrees of relevance, will be concerned with them. Similarly from the point of view of method. Although in certain fields the subject matter itself may be methods of thinking, the importance of the attitude of critical evaluation must not be lost sight of in any field. It must pervade the curriculum as the fundamental allegiance of both teacher and student. Every other commitment must be prepared to accept its challenge and undergo trial by careful scrutiny before it can be responsibly held.

A great gap has always existed between talk about critical method and its practice. Many who spoke in the past about the importance of critical method tacitly assumed that it would strengthen belief in "the truths" they inherited and weaken "the prejudices" of those who disagreed with them. But, as events put cherished beliefs into doubt, and as spokesmen for pernicious errors also invoked the shibboleths of criticism, a reaction set in. One of the noteworthy features of the "new failure of nerve" in contemporary American life is fervent *dispraise* of critical methods and attitudes towards the dominant ideals of our culture. Criticism is now often equated with negativism and defeatism. It is selling America short. From the most disparate quarters the charge has been made that the weaknesses of American education, even of American democracy, are in large measure to be laid at the door of American teachers. They are guilty of having adopted the attitude of critical objectivity in the classroom,[1] and consequently of disarming their students before the onslaughts of enemies of democracy. They are guilty of having "taught contempt and fear of truth" to an entire generation of students by insisting upon the distinction between "fact and opinion."[2]

To some extent this criticism of criticism expresses the typical war mentality observable in all countries of the world. But its roots go much deeper. Where people feel secure about their values they are less likely to be nervous when critical appraisal is made of them. The vogue of the critical attitude in some areas of American culture, literature, biography, history, reflected the degree of assurance with which the American community accepted its values. The more imperilled these values became by developments abroad and at home, the more

[1] Marie Syrkin: *Your School, Your Child* (New York: L. B. Fischer Publishing Corporation; 1944), *passim.*
[2] Mark van Doren: *Liberal Education* (New York: Henry Holt & Company; 1943), p. 177.

urgent became the need for clarification, restatement, and re-dedication. Unfortunately, this need was met by dogmatic and hysterical reaffirmation of slogans whose vagueness had been a target of previous attack. The earlier critics began to be blamed for the conditions they described. In a prolonged spell of bad weather, people become irritated by the weatherman. Under social conditions of tension and conflict, uncertainty often provokes a response of fear rather than of inquiry.

For present purposes, I am not concerned with the causes of the distrust of criticism but with the validity of the current arguments against it, and against the alleged overemphasis on *methods* of thinking in education. For reasons that will soon appear, I shall use the terms "critical method" and "scientific method" interchangeably. I shall consider four general lines of argument that have been advanced against the view that scientific method should be central in the modern educational curriculum. (1) Concern with scientific method tends to create a mood of wholesale skepticism, of exaggerated distrust and cynical debunking. (2) Sensitiveness to the continuity of scientific inquiry, to the tentative and probable character of conclusions won by it, begets an indifference to programs of action: it is incompatible with a firm stand on basic problems of our culture whose consideration we have been urging as subject matter of the modern curriculum. (3) Preoccupation with method spells the death of vision and a creeping paralysis of the creative centers of mental life: it may inspire a passion for clarity but, in the words of a French critic, it is "the shining clarity of empty glasses." (4) Truth has many mansions, and scientific truth is one of its lowliest stories: there is some knowledge which is not accessible to scientific method, and to deny this is to become victimized by the unintelligent cult of "scientism."

1. The attack upon critical or scientific method as making for skepticism derives whatever plausibility it has by confusing

skepticism or rejection of *specific* conclusions with skepticism of "things in general"—where the latter phrase stands for all beliefs which are precious to the person making the charge. Scientific method is then conceived as a threat to those private or collective sanctities of faith, hope, and wish which depend on belief. The prospect of an education which would make the use of scientific method habitual induces a pervasive sense of uneasiness, a fear of an intellectual anarchy or nihilism that would call all things into question. And yet it should be plain that scientific method cannot establish any attitude of wholesale skepticism. For, whenever it doubts, denies, or rejects a belief, it must have *positive* grounds for the doubt, denial, or rejection. We cannot doubt all our beliefs at once, although no particular belief is beyond doubt. Charles Peirce's criticism of Descartes on this point is definitive.

What has sometimes been called skepticism is a demand for further analysis, and a confession of uncertainty as to whether a customarily accepted analysis is correct. In one sense we know that one proposition is true and another false, that one act is better than another, that one woman is more beautiful than another, without knowing the correct analysis of "truth," "goodness," and "beauty." To infer that, because we regard some particular analysis of the *concept* of truth or justice inadequate, we are therefore calling into question the existence of truths and just actions, is preposterous. One of the ways of determining the adequacy of any such analysis is whether it squares with what we can observe by close study of judgments and actions which are warranted true and just by evidence at hand.

No one resents demands for evidence concerning matters about which he cares little. And one positively welcomes them in fields in which he is confident that he has knowledge. But it is quite different when we are challenged about precious beliefs to which we are emotionally wedded and for which rational grounds are not easy to find. Everyone holds some beliefs for which no rational grounds can be given. But few are willing to admit that they do—particularly when these beliefs are regarded as important. This reluctance is the unconscious tribute that men pay to their own rationality—acquired though it be.

The comforting assurance which fundamental beliefs give us is derived from their sway as familiar habits. To rest such beliefs on logical grounds, especially when we have not previously sought or formulated these grounds, is to place them on something precarious. It is to put in risk something which because of habit we do not feel is a risk. But the consequence of putting them in risk may be to weaken the passional force of belief and introduce an uneasiness whose edge may gradually weaken our emotional certainties. There is, for example, an important strand in the Christian tradition from St. Augustine down, which is suspicious of any attempt to base belief in the existence of God on logical reasons alone. God's existence seems more incontrovertible to some believers than the reasons which would justify their belief in Him. Since no one grasps all the implications of reasons, no one can be safeguarded from surprises—among which may be some that would testify *against* the belief in God.

The current dispraise of criticism is born out of the fear that it imperils not the existence of God but the validity of democracy. Yet it is clear that most current theoretical criticisms of democracy are as old as Plato. What gave these criticisms force in the eyes of many were not additional arguments but the threatening practical successes of totalitarianism. Faint hearts and weak minds in democratic countries were impressed by triumphant power in the most vulgar way. They attributed this power in large measure to the absence of criticism, and imagined that existing democracies could become just as powerful as their rivals if all tendencies towards criticism were burned away in a faith every whit as fanatical as the faiths of the enemies of democracy.

It was this superficial assumption—one actually incompatible with the rationale and spirit of democracy—that accounted for a misunderstanding of the whole drift of criticism in the few regions of American culture in which it appeared. Criticisms were rarely launched against democracy, but against practices and conditions that belied the democratic ideal. Criticism was directed against the duplicity of slogans, the miscarriage of justice, and the cruelties of unnecessary poverty. In the nature of the case, such criticism could have no sustained force unless it was based on fact rather than skepticism, on a commitment to some values rather than others. A mood of general skepticism would have blunted its impact. There may have been disproportions of emphasis, lack of historical perspective and balance. *There were cases in which criticism was dishonest; particularly when American democracy was damned for its slightest lapse while critics ignored by discreet silence, when they did not praise, monstrous crimes in their favorite dictatorship.* But this was not skepticism—rather a mixture of credulity and duplicity. On the whole, criticism was motivated by a desire to achieve clarity, consistency, and truth.

The discomfiture produced by critical analysis and "exposures" arose from a fear that what was said about the deficiencies of American democracy, and about the gap between professions and performance, might be true. The *existence* of these truths might give aid and comfort to the enemies of democracy. But the *recognition* of these truths by democrats could have no such effect, particularly when coupled with a recognition of the truths about totalitarian countries.

No one has presented convincing evidence that American students were indifferent to democratic ideals because of their addiction to critical methods of thought. For one thing, this would be difficult to do until we had some evidence that more than a small number of students had actually acquired the habits of critical thought. What is called "debunking" is a substitution of one form of dogmatism for another. It substitutes for the notion that some men are angelic mutants the notion that all men are but ignoble variants of one type. It has nothing to do with criticism which consists of the attempt to distinguish between what makes sense and what does not, and of the examination of evidence to determine whether what makes sense is true or false, and *how* true or false.

The belief that faith in democracy can be instilled by the same methods as faiths in other forms of society overlooks the distinctive character of the democratic faith. This lies in its assumption that the reasonableness of the democratic way of life may be established by open, critical inquiry of its consequences. The *initial* loyalty to democracy, like the initial loyalty to anything else, arises from social atmosphere and practice. *Rational* loyalty results from a critical consideration of the claims, achievements, and shortcomings of democracy compared to those of its rivals. The practice of democracy comes first in the order of time; the justification of democracy comes first in the order of logic. By training its students to think critically, a democracy gives them the power and the right to evaluate democracy, confident that its claims will withstand the analysis—that initial loyalties will become transformed into rational loyalties. No other form of society dares to chance this.

This means that ultimately a democracy is committed to facing the truth about itself. Preaching and edification have their holiday uses but they do not inspire initial loyalty—only practice does—nor do they sustain loyalty against critical doubts, for they present no rational grounds. It is in the very process of public, critical thinking that the democratic community and scientific community meet. Whoever introduces a breach in this process offends against both. Scientific skepticism in any specific situation flowers from a seed which is love of truth. A democracy is the only society which in principle believes that men can accept the truth in every realm of thought, and live with it.

2. The purpose of thinking is to reach conclusions. The validity of any specific conclusion depends upon the methods by which it is reached. Upon what does the validity of the methods depend? Without fear of circularity, we can say that these methods are justified by their historical fruitfulness in the solution of problems. That is why in any specific inquiry we are more likely to judge whether a problem is truly solved by reference to the methods of inquiry that have been followed, than we are to evaluate these methods by a *specific* result. This explains why we do not abandon the methods of scientific medicine when confronted by a patient who has been cured by an incantation after he has been given up by the physicians.

It also illumines the familiar contrast between "*how* we think" and "*what* we think." The *how* of thinking is more important than the *what* of thinking, not because the two are separable, for the *how* refers to the *what* in a class of cases or situations, but because it stresses the habits and morals of thought upon which the quest for truth and its successive corrections depend. Nonetheless, despite the self-corrective procedure of science, it always gives us a conclusion to a *specific* problem even if it is no more than that no warranted conclusion can be drawn. Many who complain about the footlessness of thought would do well to ascertain first whether thinking is going on.

The fear that stress upon critical methods of thinking will weaken desire to reach positive conclusions often reflects the failure to understand that genuine thinking is not a process of free association but departs from a specific problem that controls it. The solution of the problem is the goal even when the means at hand are not adequate or when its low degree of urgency allows the quest for a solution to be postponed. Nor is there any ground for the assumption that, because scientific method does not warrant solutions that are certain, it does not warrant solutions that are *sufficient* for action, resolute action. The quaintness of this assumption is apparent not only in the light of the revolutionary achievements of science, which makes no claim to certainty, but in the light of every practical art, from medicine to military welfare, where resoluteness of action often goes hand in hand with a conclusion whose probabilities just shade those of its alternative.

There is nothing in the emphasis on scientific method in education which forbids reaching conclusions or making recommendations. There are occasions when *not* to do so would betray its spirit. The refusal to assert conclusions as warranted or to take a pragmatic stand on controversial issues is sometimes justified because of the necessity of avoiding "indoctrination" in the classroom. This subject calls for a few words.

Any discussion of indoctrination, if it is to avoid confusion and interminable verbalism, must distinguish between the nature of indoctrination and its justification. By "indoctrination" I mean the process of teaching through which acceptance of belief is induced by nonrational or irrational means, or both.

Nonrational methods of inducing belief involve the use of the technique of conditioning. Since it is necessary for human beings when they are young to act upon beliefs long before they can possibly understand or justify them, indoctrination is so far unavoidable. Since this is not a controversial point, the issue must be sought elsewhere. Children will be indoctrinated in *some* specific beliefs, but the relevant questions are *which* beliefs and *who* is to determine them. To take the last question first: are these beliefs to depend exclusively on the authority of the community or also on that of educators? We have already indicated our answer: in a democracy the social and moral ideals of the community are filtered through the critical consciousness of its educators. This provides a clue to the distinctive quality of the beliefs and habits, like kindness, cleanliness, etc., in which children are to be "indoctrinated": they are to be such that a rational justification of them *can* be given on another level. But at *every* level the individual's power of reflective thought is to be encouraged and developed, so that when he reaches intellectual maturity he will be able to assess for himself the validity of the beliefs and habits in which he has been indoctrinated. *In the educational system of a democracy, the authority of method must ultimately replace the authority of persons and institutions in the determination of truth.* "Ultimately" here suggests not the postponement of critical education to some fixed period but the continuation of a process begun as the child's intelligence emerges and develops in power.

Indoctrination by *irrational means,* as distinct from non-rational means, is the art of inducing consent, not by the techniques of conditioning, but by "argument" that has the appearance of reason. The objection to indoctrination of this kind is not that it reaches conclusions. The conclusions may be true. It is to the methods by which they are reached. But it is an insuperable objection. Even if a conclusion is known to be true on other grounds, there is no justification for "putting it over" by sophism, one-sided presentation, or cooked evidence. The enormity of the offence in teaching of this kind is not mitigated by the sincerity of the person indoctrinating or by the fact that he may be unconscious of what he is doing. It is bad teaching, and no one who persists in it belongs in the classroom.

It is sometimes asked: how is indoctrination to be recognized? In general by the same tokens by which we recognize propaganda. The most obvious sign of indoctrination, as of propaganda which professes to reach conclusions by argument, is not outright invention but suppression of evidence that tends to invalidate or weaken a favored conclusion. No one objects to the teachers of natural science reaching and defending conclusions in class. Indeed, it would be ridiculous if they did not. We do not fear indoctrination here. We are confident that if the teacher employs scientific methods, students will be apprised of whatever evidence exists that testifies against the hypothesis under consideration.

The social sciences are different. Their subject matter is so loaded with value judgments, they engage such strong emotions, that we cannot rely on the automatic operation of the method of disinterested inquiry. Even the well-intentioned teacher may not be aware he is indoctrinating, or prejudicing the analysis. The best working rule here is for the teacher to deliberately build up the case for the position he is arguing against or cannot himself accept. He should strive to do it in such a way that reasonable proponents of the position will accept it as a fair exposition of their views—and then, and only then, let loose his critical shafts against it. It requires pedagogic skill to do this, but nothing less will insure the students against a pet phobia or enthusiasm. *No matter how controversial a subject may be, the teacher is justified in reaching or stating conclusions provided he has honestly made accessible to students the relevant data and arguments of the conflicting positions.* This is a permissive, not a compulsive condition, of course. If he is interested in teaching, as well as in the promulgation of what he believes to be the truth, he will make the discussion of a controversial subject an occasion for co-operative thinking. Where there is a danger that students may make the teacher's position their own because of the prestige he enjoys, or where students are apparently shopping around for something consoling to believe no matter what its source or validity, the teacher does well *not* to express his personal stand—convinced as he may be of it.

Each generation of students has its own dogmas which it takes for granted. Whatever else a teacher does, he must make his students aware of these dogmas, that there are alternatives to them, and that they must assume an intellectual and moral responsibility for their first principles.

But if among these first principles there are value judgments, how is it possible to avoid on the one hand indoctrination and on the other a pallid neutrality—or, what is worse, uneasy silence before the earnest questions of life? The detailed answer must be reserved until we consider the question of value judgments in education. It is sufficient here to say that, except for those who are prepared to acknowledge that their value judgments are arbitrary, it is possible to show that value judgments like other judgments may be reached without indoctrination.

3. Perhaps the most widespread objection against emphasis on critical method in education, and in culture generally, is that it militates against vision. To stop up the organs of vision is really sinning against the light. If critical education resulted in turning the intelligence merely into an efficient cleanser, it would soon have nothing left to work on. As Whitehead has put it, "If men cannot live on bread alone, still less can they do so on disinfectants."[3]

The seer of true visions, like the moral prophet, cannot be honored too much. He is always in the forefront of a new intellectual movement. An attitude that would silence him or give his pronouncements anything less than a respectful hearing condemns itself. But we honor the seer not for his vision but for the truth of his vision, and truth is often hidden at the bottom of a well. There has never been a time in which there has been a dearth of visionaries. Almost always, their visions are used as evidence for views about man and society which are incompatible with each other. Seers and prophets are notoriously at odds with their predecessors and contempo-

[3] Alfred North Whitehead: *Science and the Modern World* (New York: The Macmillan Company; 1925), pp. 83-4.

raries. To discover which is the trustworthy vision is therefore an absolute necessity for those who would put their faith in true vision. This can only be done by applying critical method to vision. To turn around at this juncture and accuse those who employ such methods of being hostile to vision is hardly just.

Criticism that is unwise, criticism that is fierce and tendentious, criticism that has the impact of a physical assault, that is commanded by a party line or is a tactic in the strategy of an intellectual pogrom, can choke off the sources of vision in others. Not all seers and prophets are tough, and in a time of troubles we hear only of those who are capable of martyrdom. But such criticism is *bad* criticism—in one sense, not criticism at all. Its proper alternative is not the absence of criticism but criticism appropriate to its subject, and guided primarily by love of truth.

The point of the objection to the educational emphasis on criticism is that it tends to make those who employ it infertile. The eye for weaknesses in other people's creations turns inward and like a lethal x-ray kills the fancies and hunches and vague perceptions struggling to be born. The result of an educational program that strengthened critical faculties might be the generation of a pack of watchdogs who frightened one another from taking the ventures and risks without which we have no use for watchdogs.

It is an open question whether the *cultivation* of critical methods has a tendency to paralyze vision and creative effort. There are, of course, great creative minds who are also masters of criticism. Almost every great creative figure in the history of philosophy has been a penetrating critic of the ideas of other philosophers. Among lesser figures, it is true that some men of great critical gifts have had very little to say in constructive solutions of philosophical problems. But in such cases it would be very difficult to establish that the weakness of constructive vision has been a *consequence* of cultivation of criticism.

Those who lie in wait merely in order to pounce upon the shortcomings of other people's visions have been cursed by nature, not by their critical art. They lack either the power of vision or the courage to back their visions, and so are reduced to perpetual exercises in immediate inferences. They are critical only because they are barren: they are not barren because they are critical. And like trainers who cannot themselves fight, like art critics who cannot paint and teachers who cannot sing—by their critical insight they can often be of great help to those who can.

That a good critic discourages himself and others from attempting creation is dubious. That he has an encouraging effect in deepening perception and insight, and indirectly affecting the standards of creation, is less dubious. That nonsense is less likely to get itself accepted as truth where the critical spirit flourishes is not dubious at all. And it remains true that good criticism must nourish itself on the existing models of excellence in thought and expression. If it does not know the labors and joys of creation, it can at least savor to the full the pleasure of understanding.

4. The charge that reliance upon scientific method is a cult of "scientism" which impoverishes human experience by stripping it of all save quantitative dimensions, treats human beings as if they were inanimate things, and systematically obscures the difference between ends and means, values and facts, derives whatever force it has from a double confusion. It confuses scientific method as a general pattern of inquiry whenever we seek knowledge, with scientific method as the procedures pursued in the study of nature, and confuses these procedures with the specific methods and techniques employed in physics.

Scientific method was not discovered in the modern world. It was implicitly followed wherever men were able to distinguish between effective and ineffective means for the accomplishment of their daily tasks. Its systematic application to nature, the formulation of its rationale, and the program of its extension to society and man—these are the distinctive contributions of the modern world. Far from imperilling human values, scientific method enables us to give them a more effective status in experience. It is not the whole of life, but in its broadest sense it encompasses the whole intellectual enterprise of man. Those who urge its centrality in the educational curriculum do not seek to narrow the course of studies to the natural or social sciences but to enrich it by bringing the method to bear on all subject matters. Nor do they rule out or disparage the experiences of appreciation of color, sound, form, and feeling. They assume that the more we understand, the more we appreciate; and that *tested* understanding always reveals the *pattern* of scientific method. It is not fortuitous that the author of *Logic: The Theory of Inquiry* is the author of *Art as Experience* and *Democracy and Education*, and that he has unweariedly insisted upon distinguishing between the general scientific method of handling subject matter, and some specific subject matter which illustrates the method in a particular way.

There are those who would restrict the term [science] to mathematics or to disciplines in which exact results can be determined by rigorous methods of demonstration. Such a conception limits even the claims of physics and chemistry to be sciences, for according to it, the only scientific portion of these subjects is the strictly mathematical. The position of what are ordinarily termed the biological sciences is even more dubious, while social subjects and psychology would hardly rank as sciences at all, when measured by this definition. Clearly we must take the idea of science with some latitude. The important thing is to discover those traits in virtue of which various fields are called scientific. When we raise the question in this way we are led to put emphasis upon *methods of dealing* with subject-matter rather than to look for uniform objective traits in subject-matter. From this point of view science signifies . . . the existence of systematic methods of inquiry, which when they are brought to bear on a range of facts, enables us to understand them better and to control them more intelligently, less haphazardly, and with less routine.[4]

The chief features of the scientific method of dealing with subject matter are well known. They are the recognition and definition of a problem, the formulation of an hypothesis, the elaboration of its logical implications, the performance of an experimental act, and the observation of its consequences. The experimental act does not necessarily mean a laboratory experiment. It may involve no more than the use of a tool, a change in the position of the body, or just looking—*all under critical controls*—depending upon the character of the problem. The observation does not have to be quantitatively measurable in any exact way. Even in many of the sciences, observation contents itself with gross occurrence, and in ordinary affairs this is usually sufficient. Every step in the pattern of inquiry may be an occasion for special analysis. Dialectic, analysis of meaning, and what is usually designated by formal logic are here conceived as part of the pattern—an indispensable part but one which by itself does not suffice to give us knowledge of fact.

To many there seems to be something awkward about the term "scientific" when used to describe a method applied to humanistic or literary subject matter, but the exact equivalent of the term in these fields is "critical." An historian, for example, may deny that there is any such thing as "scientific" history or that there can be. But no historian will admit that he is writing fiction, or deny that some historical accounts are more warranted than others, or fail to repudiate the notion that he is writing uncritically. Yet precisely those features in

[4] John Dewey: *Sources of a Science of Education* (New York: Liveright Publishing Corporation; 1929), p. 8ff. My italics.

an historical account which distinguish it from fiction, which make it more or less warranted than another account, which testify to its critical rather than uncritical nature, are features that will be found to be part of the general pattern of scientific inquiry. The same is true for anything put forth as a valid interpretation of a work of art or a correct explication of a text, without in any way denying that different qualities of experience are present, and that the critical or scientific approach has additional functions quite different in deciphering the meanings of a poem from, say, reconstructing the skeleton of a prehistoric animal from a few fragments of bone.

The great challenge to the centrality of scientific method in the process of education arises from the presence of values. How, on this view, are they to be approached? Can they be understood, can they be evaluated, without breaking free from the general pattern of inquiry? To this I now turn.

No matter what his *theory* of value is, every educator is committed to the proposition that one of the tasks of education is to teach values. Since not all values can be taught, and some selection must be made, every educator assumes that some values are better than others. What does it mean to teach values? What does it mean to teach that some values are better than others?

To teach values properly is to do a variety of related things. First, it is to make students *aware* of their attitudes of preference expressed in their choices and organized in their habits. By the time an individual reaches the stage when he can differentiate between himself and others he already has acquired a whole set of values. Every child imbibes values as he learns how to speak; and he learns how to speak before he learns how to think. By the time he is confronted by an experience that provokes moral doubt he is already in possession of many values. He does not start from scratch. He is committed to many values that may be more eloquently attested in his behavior than in his speech. These values are rarely organized and even their conflicts seldom lead to clear articulation unless certain intellectual habits have already been acquired. The existence of these values, rather than their source, is the important thing to note for our subsequent analysis.

To teach values is not only to make students aware of their commitments. It is also to make them aware of attitudes of evaluation to which not they but *others* are committed. This is not easily done. For it requires more than the realization that their own value commitment formally excludes its opposite. If they recognize themselves as ambitious, they must, of course, also be capable of formally recognizing what it means to be not ambitious. But this is not enough by far. For to be properly aware of what it means to be not ambitious is to understand it in relation to the psychological, historical, social, or other contexts which make *that* commitment as natural or plausible to the person who holds it as being ambitious is to oneself. Here a good teacher working with good books in the fields of literature and history can make the value commitments of others appear as vital options, actively competing with the students' own, instead of abstract negations. If we want to understand what "intolerance" means, we must make some historical or literary character who was self-righteously intolerant come alive. Assuming for the moment that our values are "goods"—I am trying to use language innocently— we must make the "bads" credible in the sense that imaginatively we can conceive ourselves holding them.

Finally, to teach values means to develop within students a willingness to commit themselves to new values, and to reaffirm or to reject the values to which they find themselves previously committed. When this is done after the value alternatives which are being excluded have been presented, then it can be said we are teaching that some values are better than others. When this willingness is developed by rhetoric and the hortatory arts, by promises of personal reward or fear of punishment, we have indoctrination. When this willingness results from a rational consideration of the evidence for one or the other commitment, then we have scientific determination of value judgments.

The retort comes at once: then in either case indoctrination is unavoidable, for there is no way of establishing scientifically that one judgment of value is better or truer than another without circularity. Only judgments of fact can be established scientifically.

The view that what is generically called scientific method, as distinct from the specific techniques of the special sciences, is irrelevant in establishing the validity of judgments of value, is what unites all philosophers—whether Thomist or narrow positivist, whether intuitionist or reductive materialist—against the experimentalist philosophy. To do justice to the claims and criticisms of these various schools of ethical thought would require a treatise. But I propose in lieu of this to outline in a positive way an experimental approach to value judgments insofar as they enter into the content of education, and to see how far it will carry us before differences in philosophical theory obtrude.

A scientific or rational approach to judgments of value consists in (a) the investigation of the causes of such judgment, (b) their logical implications, and (c) their probable consequences. This investigation is always to be undertaken in relation to alternative values which limit freedom of choice.

(a) That judgments of value have histories, that they are related to interests, that they grow out of *problems* of valuation and appraisal are truths that no one denies. What is often denied is the relevance of these factors to the specific quality of value in any situation. Yet we are all aware of the simple fact that knowledge of the causes of value judgment often aids us in understanding what we are valuing. All who are not theoretically doctrinaire will grant that our knowledge that this man is starving makes some difference to our understanding of the good and bad quality of an action that flows from his acute need.

To discover why a man comes to value what he does, does not necessarily lead us to justify his value, but it enables us to be more intelligent about its character. What is true for individual values is true for group values. The whole of modern anthropology consists in removing the shock of difference, when one value system is confronted with another, by providing the cultural and historical perspectives within which both are surveyed—not rationalized—as responses to some need. One of the differences between moral insularity and parochialism on the one hand, and moral sophistication and wisdom on the other, is that the latter is aware of the conditions out of which values grow. We may not countenance these values when we have such knowledge; but we at least are not completely baffled by them. We know what they are an outgrowth of and response to.

(b) Value judgments are understood not only through knowledge of their origins and causes but through knowledge of their structural interrelations. What does it mean to say that an action is "courageous," "loyal," or "just"? Each value has a quality that we experience as specifically its own, but the meaning of the quality is enriched by the perception of the relations it bears to other values. Values come in clusters and constellations. They supplement and complement each other like colors. The *interpretation* of the nature of the relations between values may depend upon conflicting theories of their ontological, psychological and social status. But the *existence* of these relations has been recognized by thinkers as far apart as Aristotle and Pascal, Scheler and Dewey. Because these relationships are general, they are never sufficient in enabling us to grasp the meaning of the value qualities in any specific situation. Nonetheless, they contribute to enlarging our understanding and sharpening our perceptions in particular cases. When we are familiar with the ways in which values call to values, we know what to look for, what to reinforce or guard against, what to affirm or reject.

We have called this immanent relationship between values logical. It might just as well be called dramatic. For it involves the conflict and clash or reinforcement and support of human attitudes as they develop in time. This development is funded in the meanings of the values. The analysis of value relations therefore discloses something significant about the history and nature of men.

(c) The third avenue to an understanding of values is perhaps the most important. It consists in grasping the consequences of judgments proposing that something should be done, anticipating their effects on the original difficulties which set the problem of moral choice, and noting their bearing upon other values to which we are implicitly committed. To ignore or discount the consequences of a proposed course of conduct is the mark of fanaticism. And even fanatics often pretend that they have taken the costs of their actions into consideration. But these other values to which we are committed—are they not finally valid independent of consequences? No—they can be challenged, too, if a problem arises about them. And if we take our problems, as we should, one at a time, and remember that a moral problem is created not merely by asking a question but by discovering an objective difficulty in a concrete situation, we avoid narrow circularity and a vicious infinite regress. Whether life is worth living is a serious and legitimate question under certain circumstances when honor or health are at stake, but it is frivolous to introduce it as if it were necessarily involved in every moral problem that arises. Those who believe that all value deliberation *must* at some point anchor itself to ultimate or intrinsic values which are beyond all possibility of scientific validation are as mistaken as those who hold that scientific judgments of fact *must* be based upon incontrovertible first truths for which no evidence can be given.[5]

The advantages of this approach to value judgments are independent of the specific analysis of the nature of value judgments. Whether we consider them as descriptions in the indicative mood, or commands in the imperative mood, or wishes in the optative mood, is not as important as that we should be able to answer the question "*Why?*" about them and uncover the nexus of relations, of causes and consequences, which makes one judgment, command, or wish more reasonable than another.

This does not in the least deny that there is a distinction between our knowledge of what it is right to do and our attitude toward the doing of it. Many who are aware of the injustice of racial discrimination are unable to liberate themselves from what they admit to be unfounded prejudice. The problem of inducing a change in attitude, of bridging the gap between recognition of moral truth and practical acceptance, is a perennial and basic educational task. Modern psychology has contributed powerful techniques of effecting voluntary persuasion that bear on this problem. But the point I wish to stress is that the transformation of attitude, no matter how subtly undertaken, is logically completely subordinate to the discovery of moral truth. Otherwise we have not risen above the level of non-rational indoctrination.

Nor am I denying that a legitimate distinction can be drawn between the judgments of fact and the judgments of value based upon them. But the stress should be placed upon their interrelation in any specific problem of evaluation, and above all on the method by which evaluations are justified. Whether this method is called "critical," "scientific," "experimental," or "rational" is a matter of indifference. The significant issue is whether in reaching conclusions regarded as true in consider-

[5] Cf. Chapter vii, "Standards, Ends and Means," of my book, *John Dewey: An Intellectual Portrait* (New York: John Day Co.; 1939).

ing questions of value we depart from the basic pattern observable in reaching conclusions regarded as true in considering questions of fact.

One fundamental cleavage on this point is between those who believe that moral statements are really not cognitive assertions at all and those who believe they are. The first denies that the term "truth" has any intelligible meaning when applied to moral statements. But they exempt all moral judgments which can be construed as instrumental or purposive and limit their taboo only to statements concerning "ultimate" or "intrinsic" values. For educational uses there is a sufficient margin of agreement between these two philosophical schools as to what can be investigated and what not, to justify a common procedure. For as we have seen it is one of the hypotheses of the experimentalists that all statements which invoke "ultimate" values will be found to be instrumental or purposive in concrete situations involving other values.

Another fundamental cleavage divides those who believe that value statements are cognitive. The first maintain that the pattern of confirmation is, in essentials, the same as that which obtains in scientific inquiry. The second asserts that the pattern is different; that "scientific" inquiry into values is relevant only to the contexts of values, not to their essential qualities; and that these are authenticated by a direct intuitive grasp. The opposition between these two approaches is unbridgeable on a theoretical level. Nonetheless, here too a theoretical impasse need not hold up educational co-operation. Practice can be based on a minimum agreement. Supernaturalists, traditionalists and a priorists in insisting that *something more* is required than investigation into causes, structure, and consequences of values need not necessarily be opposed to such investigation. If it doesn't take us far enough there will be sufficient opportunity to try other methods. But a *beginning* can be made with such investigation without prejudging the theoretical issue. Those who believe that one common pattern of inquiry operates in all fields of investigation will be content to abide by the educative effects of the investigation they propose. All they ask is that the obstacles to such investigation be removed, and that it be wholeheartedly undertaken in fields in which it has hitherto been taboo.

It must be frankly recognized that this proposal is not innocent and that it will be fought tooth and nail by groups who hold to beliefs that are allegedly inaccessible to investigation by critical method but which in actuality may be affected once the authority of method replaces the authority of creed—religious, social, or political. Surely there is an inconsistency in maintaining that certain truths are beyond reach of, or comparison with, truths established by scientific method, and refusing to permit them to be investigated scientifically. For by definition they cannot be imperilled by this approach. Such opposition raises the suspicion that these beliefs may in fact be invalid and that those who are fearful of the *attempt* to approach them scientifically are fearful of their possible invalidity.

If we conceive of science, as John Dewey has suggested, in terms of methods of dealing with subject matter instead of uniform traits of subject matter, we can establish the living bond between the scientific and liberal spirit. This lies not in the methods of physics, or the methods of the humanities, but in the method of intelligence which uses the devices and techniques appropriate to specific subject matters. Method is central in a liberal philosophy as in science because it undercuts the absolutisms that would arrest the flow of new knowledge and new insights. Method should be central in educational activity because it not only evaluates the funded tradition of the past but enhances the capacity to enrich it. This is the meaning of liberalism in education. "Like science,"

writes Morris R. Cohen, "liberalism insists on a critical examination of the content of all our beliefs, principles, or initial
hypotheses and on submitting them to a continuous process of
verification so that they will be progressively better founded
in experience and reason."[6]

---

[6] Morris R. Cohen, "What I Believe," *The Nation,* Vol. 133, No. 3448
(August 5, 1931), p. 130.

Chapter 8

A PROGRAM FOR
EDUCATION

---

*"The mind does not live by instruction.
It is no prolix gut to be stuffed."*
WOODROW WILSON

ONE OF the most furious controversies in contemporary education is being waged over a false issue. This is the issue of required curriculums versus elective curriculums, prescription or free choice in education. One group maintains not only that a liberal education in a democracy should contain certain required *studies* but that this requirement entails a curriculum of completely prescribed *courses* for all students. The second group maintains that since a basic moral principle of democracy is equality of concern for all persons to realize their best capacities, and since individual needs, interests, and talents vary considerably, therefore to prescribe knowledge of certain subject matters and facility in certain skills for all students is to run counter to the philosophy of democracy.

In both cases the argument starts from true premises but reaches false conclusions.

The strongest proponents of an all-prescribed curriculum are members of the Hutchins-Adler-Barr school of educational thought. A few representative citations give their position.

A genuine curriculum will permit no student to miss any important thing anywhere; the whole of it will be prescribed, and prescribed for everybody . . . if liberal education is, it is the same for everybody; . . . the training it requires, in addition to being formal, should be homogeneous through four years—if the best is known, there is no student whom it will not fit, and each should have all of it. [van Doren][1]

The abolition of the elective system goes to the very heart of the problem. Liberal education is developed only when a curriculum can be devised which is the same for all men. . . . [M. Adler][2]

Education for Freedom is the same for all men, and all men must, alike have it . . . a free society cannot be based upon an elective system of teaching. All the people must study the same lessons. [A. Meiklejohn][3]

In previous chapters I have argued that there are certain skills and bodies of subject matter whose study should be required of all students. The character of this prescription differs profoundly from what educators of this school believe to be the minimum indispensables of a liberal education. But even if we accept the notion that a liberal education should be classical and formal, it is a fateful logical mistake to deduce therefrom that *a specific curriculum of courses be required for everybody*. No matter what the desirable studies in a democracy are conceived to be, the specific *courses* of study best adapted to give some mastery of these studies is an experimental question to be decided from time to time, from country to country, and from institution to institution.

Let us borrow a metaphor from Plato and Aristotle to make this clear. They often compare goodness of the soul, which the educator aims to develop, with the health of the body, which the physician aims to help us achieve. Now the elements of

[1] Mark van Doren: *Liberal Education* (New York: Henry Holt & Company; 1943), pp. 117, 110.
[2] MBS radio broadcast, under the auspices of Education for Freedom, Inc., February 7, 1944.
[3] MBS radio broadcast, under the auspices of Education for Freedom, Inc., February 14, 1944.

health are the same for everybody. We can indicate the conditions which must be satisfied before any individual can be declared healthy. That is to say, the formal criterion or definition of health is the same for everybody—namely, certain optimum levels of physical and mental activity. But would a scientific physician prescribe the *same* regimen, the *same* diet, the *same* medication for *all* individuals independently of their history, their constitution, and their specific deficiencies? Such procedure is an unfailing sign of a quack. Similarly, it smacks of educational quackery to demand that, because the elements of a good education in a democracy should be the same for everyone, everyone should get it in the *same* way, by the *same* courses, in the *same* time and order, independently of differences in aptitude, interests, and past educational experience. One would imagine, in view of these differences in personality and background, that identical methods and curriculums are hardly likely to lead to identical results, and that the more uniform we wish the educational *achievement* of students to be, the more varied and flexible our methods and curriculums must be[4] without denying the likelihood that they will exhibit certain constant features.

It may be asked, returning to our metaphor, is it not possible to find a diet that would be good for all men in the sense that we could indicate the optimum diet of proteins, carbohydrates, fats, minerals, and vitamins which would best further health? Certainly, but note that such a diet cannot be deduced from a formal definition of health, that it may be found in a wide variety of different foods, and that it can be combined with favorite foods they enjoy for reasons other than health. But even more important, it may turn out that there is no one optimum health diet for everybody everywhere, although the formal definition of health is the same, for it may be a function of social and cultural factors whose changes vitally affect

[4] John Dewey: *Education Today* (New York: G. P. Putnam's Sons; 1940), p. 273.

what enters into such a diet. This point is very effectively made by the noted anthropologist, Bronislaw Malinowski, in his discussion of the meaning of the expression "human nature."

The nutritive specialist can define the optimum of a diet in terms of proteins, carbohydrates, mineral salts and vitamins necessary for the maintenance of the human organism in good health. This optimum, however, must be defined with reference to a given culture. For the optimum is only definable with relation to the amount of labor, muscular and nervous, to the complexity of the tasks, to potential strains and efforts demanded by a given cultural configuration from its members. At the same time, the ideal formula provided by a dietician is of no practical or theoretical importance unless we can relate it to environmental supplies, to the systems of production and possibilities of distribution.[5]

The principle involved here is applicable to education, too, and shows how hazardous it is to lay down an ideal education for all men, at all times, everywhere. It is possible to discover the minimum essentials of a good education for all men within a certain period of a given culture, and to justify it empirically, as we have tried to do. But, as we shall see, this is only the beginning.

We must therefore conclude that the whole issue as described by partisans of the school of thought under consideration has been misconceived. They formulate the question in a manner that would force us to choose between an all-prescribed, all-canned curriculum on the one hand, and an all-elective, all-confused curriculum on the other hand. But these do not exhaust the alternatives. We reject both. Recognizing that *all* citizens in a democratic community are entitled to the best education available, and assuming that the required essentials of a best education are as we have described them, the task

[5] Bronislaw Malinowski: *A Scientific Theory of Culture and Other Essays* (ed. Huntington Cairns; Chapel Hill: University of North Carolina Press; 1944), pp. 79–80.

of educators is, through intelligent and sympathetic *guidance*, to provide the specific and appropriate means to give each person the best education he can get. In carrying out this task, certain procedures and curriculums will be generally valid. It is not likely that any one procedure or curriculum will be universally valid.

And why should it be, if we recognize, as democrats must, the unique qualities of individual personalities and our equal responsibility and concern for them? These qualities of personality need not be lost when they are orchestrated "into a society of free individuals in which all, through their own work, contribute to the liberation and enrichment of the lives of others."[6] Every individual has a duty to serve the community; but does it follow that all individuals must serve society in the same way? No more in the case of citizenship than of education!

Yet it does not follow from the foregoing that a sympathetic consideration of individual needs and interests precludes the necessity of requiring that students master some definite subject matters and skills. The difficulty lies in that too many traditional educators think in terms of courses rather than subject matters whereas some progressive educators have gone off the rails and assumed that because needs are personal, subject matter is personal, too. Courses and subject matters are usually related but they are not identical. To defend the required study of certain subject matters is not to assert that these subject matters are predetermined for all time and in all places, or that certain fixed courses must be the medium of their transmission. It is to assert that, given the modern world we live in and accepting the ends of education already indicated, the study of some subject matters can be shown to be necessary for all individuals. For all individuals need it. And to sharpen the

[6] Dewey: *Education Today*, p. 298.

point against some progressive educators who have subjectiv-
ized, and therefore radically distorted, the meaning of the
basic terms in their own philosophy, we may put this as follows: not only should the study of *some* subject matters be
required of all students but at least part of the requirement
should consist of the study of the *same* subject matters—again
not to be confused with identical courses and curriculums.
This common requirement is justified by common need, in the
literal distributive sense that every individual person has a need
for it.

The central word here is "need." As a term it is ambiguous
and slippery but in an educational context it can be given sufficient precision to rescue it from those who use it interchangeably with interests, preferences, likes, and desires. A need in
education is any want, absence, or lack whose fulfillment is a
necessary condition for the achievement of a desirable end. It
follows therefore that needs are *objective*, not errant offsprings
of fancy, and that they are not only individual but also *social*,
related essentially to value-norms rooted in the community. If
health is a desirable educational goal, then the needs of a
child for proper food, or for special treatment to counteract a
deficiency, are objective even if he is unaware of them. If intelligent participation in social life is desirable in a democracy,
then the needs of every student to be well-informed in certain
subject matters, to possess the skills of critical reading and
thinking, and to acquire habits of responsible action are objective, even if he is unaware of them. When these needs become
felt needs, the specific processes of interaction between the individual and his environment by which these needs are ful-
filled will be reinforced by the powers of organic impulse.
When these needs become *intelligently* felt needs, the individual displays a greater initiative and responsibility in determining the quality and direction of his educational experience. He learns more, integrates better, sees more deeply.
The drive to fill his needs becomes voluntarily sustained against

obstacles. Out of this voluntarily sustained—because intelligently felt—drive, there is born a discipline more pervasive and more reliable than any imposed by external rewards or fear of punishment.

What determines the existence of needs in the individual are natural structures and social institutions and the operation of intelligence. Their recognition, in the first instance, is the task of parent and teacher, family and school. The child, and later the student, actively co-operates in setting needs; but until full maturity is reached he cannot assume total responsibility for the decision as to what constitutes his educational needs. The realization of the importance of student co-operation, student responsibility, and self-activation in recognizing and furthering their needs, and the devising of methods for evoking this student response, have been almost wholly the work of progressive educators.

There is a common need for all individuals in a democratic community to study the subject matters and acquire the skills indicated in the previous chapters. From this it does not follow that *all* subject matters studied and *all* skills acquired should be common. For though all needs are objective, not all are universal. There are individual needs, in the sense that some individuals have them and some not, whose fulfillment is justified if we accept as a valid end of education the development of personalities capable of adding fresh insight to the accumulated stores of tradition. A mathematically gifted student, a student with a great passion for science and with capabilities to match, another with a highly developed musical ear, another with a flair for poetry or criticism, should normally not be exempt from common prescriptions; but the school has an obligation to give them special opportunities for further study commensurate with their talents and interests. Conventionally, here is where the area of election begins; actually, when the students have received the benefit of expert and sympathetic guidance, this may be called an additional, but not common, prescription. But a "prescription" whose rational justification in the light of his own needs is voluntarily accepted by the student is just as much an "elective." At any rate, the course of study for different students is not likely to be identical throughout their college career.

There is another dimension of need which is almost altogether personal and individual. It arises whenever individuals are studying together as a group, in either the prescribed or the elective areas of study. But it is crucially important in teaching studies that are required of all students. Differences in ability, desire, and emotional make-up vitally affect the extent to which the objective needs of students can be met. Anyone who has taught a class at any level, indeed anyone who, as a member of a class, has attentively observed what goes on, understands the tremendous differences in the net educational effect which result from student variation in educational background, knowledge, articulate language habits, range and depth of apprehension, zest for ideas, imagination, habits of study, and powers of memory. This is the crux of the teacher's problem even when all other educational issues are settled. It is a problem he must meet every class hour of his life. It is in the light of this problem that the most powerful arguments for progressive education can be made. Individualized instruction for every student through a tailor-made curriculum administered by one or more teachers might seem at first blush to be an ideal solution. But not only is such a plan impracticable in an era of mass education, it loses certain educational advantages derived from the give and take and cross-questioning of classroom experience.

The most adequate method of dealing with this problem is the limitation of the size of classes to a point where the teacher can learn to know each one of his students as an individual person. Through this knowledge he can supply the individual stimuli and aids that are uniquely fitted to special needs, provide opportunities for acceleration for the gifted, and at the same time keep the collective work of the group at a level from which all can profit. Whatever the philosophy, principles, and techniques of progressive education are proclaimed to be, their substance is absent when classes as a rule run to more than, say, twenty students—although there is no guarantee that it will be present when classes are of proper size. This makes education very expensive to the community. It should be. Is there anything more worthy of spending our money on? The rub is that money alone will not insure educational success.

Let us try to envisage what this means in terms of school organization, particularly on the level of liberal arts, the stronghold of educational conservatism. At once we must translate subject matters and skills into specific curriculums and courses. The translation, we shall see, is imperfect, but, unless colleges are to be conducted on the tutorial system or by the correspondence plan, courses must be one of the media of education.

1.   The liberal arts college will prescribe integrated courses in the areas of knowledge and fields of skill described in Chapter Six. We shall call this the common-core curriculum.

1.1   The content of these courses—general ideas, institutions, problems—will to a considerable degree be the same irrespective of the location of the college and its student composition.

1.2   The content of these courses, to a much lesser degree in science than in literature, to a much greater degree in social studies than in logic or ethics, will reflect differences in locality and student composition. Certain types of social problems will interest students in women's colleges, which may not arouse interest in men's colleges. There are no alternatives to the fundamental principles of physics, mathematics, and logic. In literature the patterns of excellence are so many that a considerable margin exists for variations in choice of models for study. In history, where reference to local conditions is relevant, stress and emphasis will naturally be different.

1.21 The common-core curriculum of the college will from year to year show a variation analogous to variations between the common-core curriculums of different colleges. It is assumed that the faculty in planning the common-core curriculum will keep abreast of developments in the various fields of knowledge. On fundamentals it is not likely that there will be sudden shifts.

2. Upon the presentation of evidence of special mastery and maturity, supplied by objective tests and expert guidance analysis, a part of the core curriculum may be waived. All students are to receive these tests on request.

2.1 When part of the core curriculum is waived other courses, or *directed* individual studies, are to be substituted for it.

3. Upon the conclusion of the common-core studies, which will normally take two years, students will "elect" their courses along the lines of their special interest, subject to the approval of their advisors.

3.1 Normally, the amount of directed individual study, either in the form of "honors" or tutorials, will increase in the last two years.

4. The size of all classes, except for the occasion of special lectures, will be limited to approximately twenty.

5. Classes will as a rule be conducted by the discussion and seminar method.

5.1 This rule cannot be observed in courses in science and mathematics in which the preceptorial method seems better adapted for purposes of exposition and demonstration.

5.2 Intelligent use, whenever relevant, will be made of work-experience outside of the classroom.

What are the advantages of this proposed "model"? Briefly, it makes possible the construction of a workable curriculum which combines the requirements that meet common need with flexible provisions for individual need. It recognizes that

there is a body of knowledge which all individuals who are
educable may fairly be expected to know. It recognizes, too,
that there are legitimate variations in the approach to this
body of knowledge. It relates by intelligent integration the
subject matters to be studied. It makes the student responsible
for his education *after* he has explored the required fields. His
educational decisions become more responsible. His intellectual interests may have developed to a point where they have
set up deep intellectual needs. He is not rushed through his
studies at the meteoric pace of a prodigy child or shunted away
from the discipline of classroom inquiry and face-to-face relations with the teacher and other students by comprehensive
examinations. Neither books nor examinations are substitutes
for good teachers and the experience of the classroom. A student may be able to pass a comprehensive examination in a
field and yet be unable to find an equivalent for the stimulus
and insight that a teacher may provide. The knowledge and
specific skills tested by comprehensive examinations may not
remain with the student as long as the habits of perception and
thought he may acquire in the classroom.

Institutionally, the proposed model makes it possible for
colleges to introduce curricular revisions gradually, even in
the face of academic inertia. They can start from where they
are without the costs and dangers of total transformation.[7]

---

[7] In this chapter I have drawn upon the organization and experience of
the Unified Studies Division, an experiment conducted some years ago
by the Washington Square College of Liberal Arts and Science, New
York University.

Chapter 9

EDUCATION TOWARD
VOCATION

---

*"The education of the future will in the
case of every child over a certain age,
combine productive labor with education
and athletics not merely as one of the
methods of raising social production but
as the only method of producing fully
developed human beings."*

KARL MARX[1]

NOTHING is more familiar than the contrast drawn by modern
educators between liberal education and vocational education.
But as soon as we try to track down the specific differences between them we discover that no hard and fast lines can be
drawn. Usually a liberal education is so defined that if it has
any other end beyond itself, if it involves more than the joys
of consummatory experience, it is illiberal. It thus auto-
matically excludes any activity connected with "earning one's
living." This conception reflects elements drawn from both
the Greek and Hebraic tradition. In ancient Greek society
most citizens did not have to earn their own living. The work

[1] Karl Marx: *Das Kapital* (ed. Karl Kautsky; Berlin: J. W. Dietz Verlag;
1928) Vol. 1, p. 425. In the interest of the context, I have freely rendered
"Unterricht" (literally "instruction") as "education" and "Gymnastik"
as "athletics."

of the world was performed by slaves, and concern with material *means* was the distinctive mark of the *menial* in spirit. According to the Hebraic legend, work in the sweat of his face is man's curse and punishment. With primitive tools or none at all it could hardly have been conceived differently. But it recognizes a dim way that it is work which makes man human. The knowledge to which it is counterposed is not imperfect human knowledge, laboriously acquired by a body of clay, but divine. Man is expelled from the Garden of Eden because he has sought to become like unto God: his earthly career begins with a quest of human knowledge and happiness through work.

In the modern world, liberal education has always been a serious enterprise despite the existence of some students who did not take it seriously, who regarded it as a personal adornment or a badge of social superiority. It was always connected with earning one's living, although the "livings" were of a highly selected sort. The notion that the opposite of the liberal arts were the useful arts, and that therefore the liberal arts could be designated as useless, would have been dismissed as preposterous even by the most traditional of educators. For the curriculum of the liberal arts colleges of the past few centuries trained for vocations, too. The teachers, ministers, lawyers, physicians, and better-paid public servants were largely drawn from the ranks of the college educated. A liberal arts education was in fact a sufficient preparation for many kinds of careers. Like the great medieval universities, but in lesser measure, they were really professional schools.

In the contemporary world this is still true. But it is often concealed by dubbing some careers "professions" and regarding the others as "vocations." Flatly to contrast the "professions," even when we prefix the adjective "liberal" to them, with "vocations" is to express an invidious distinction. It is derived from the scorn felt by those who imagine they use only their brain as an instrument in earning their living, toward those who seem to use only their hands. It is explained mainly by the fact that most "vocations"—in ordinary times—carry with them less power, less money, and less prestige in the eyes of the community than most professions.

When does a "vocation" become a "profession"? Take the lowly street cleaner on whom the health of our cities depends. Give him civil-service status after rigorous training and examinations, raise his income to that of college professors, provide liberal pension and retirement allowances, bestow upon him the official title of "Social Physician," deck him out in a resplendent dress uniform, and before long his "vocation" will become a "profession," too.

A liberal education should do something more than prepare the student to earn his own living. But it should at least prepare him for it. The crucial question is *how* he should be prepared. No conception of liberal education is worth a second glance which professes to be unconcerned with the quality of the life a student will lead after he is through with his formal schooling—a life in which the fruits of his schooling first become apparent. All the great educators of the modern world, despite their differences as to what constitutes the best education, agree that it should be complete in the sense that it should fit men to grapple with their duties as citizens of the community. But a citizen of the community is not only a "political" entity. He is a producer, a consumer, a potential warrior, a critic, a teacher in some respects, a learner in others. He is sometimes more of one or another. But in the life of the citizen they are all related. This thought was expressed long ago by John Milton whose conception of a "complete" education is a measure by which we may still judge what belongs to a desirable education, and how it belongs. "A complete and generous education," he said, "is one that fits a man to perform skillfully, justly and magnanimously, all the acts, both public and private, of peace and war." Vocational education is part of a complete and generous education.

The fundamental problem of vocational education today, to the extent that vocations are still available, is whether it should be considered as a form of vocational *training*, serving industry and government, or whether it should be considered as an aspect of liberal education in which preparation for careers in industry and government is justified by *both* the needs of a developing personality and the interests of the community. Here, as elsewhere, we can observe a meeting of extremes which in effect makes allies of the lily-pure academician and the tough-minded practical man. The first finds utterly distasteful the idea that vocational interests should obtrude on the course of study. In his heart he believes that students who study for any other reason save the sheer love of it degrade learning. They therewith prove themselves in his eyes to be no true students at all. The second regards liberal arts studies as irritating conventional preliminaries to useful subjects whose mastery has a cash value. Wherever possible, he seeks to give vocational courses a content that is directly relevant to the tasks that must be performed on the job. For all their opposition, both agree on sharply separating liberal from vocational study, although they differ in the grounds offered for the separation. Both are united in strong opposition to any plan to make vocational education integral to liberal education.

The type of education which today is specifically labelled "vocational" is largely job-training. Despite the war of words raging against its narrowness, it is enjoying a mushroom growth, especially in the higher reaches of the educational process. It is easy to understand this growth. School is short, life is long, and no one enjoys an enforced leisure without comforts. The desire to prepare for a dignified and well-remunerated calling is perfectly legitimate. Where it is absent, a society is in the last stages of decay. The greater are the immediate opportunities for employment, the greater is the demand for special training from industry, and the greater is the interest in vocational subjects among students, particularly among those who are unhappy with the traditional course of liberal education and, as they quaintly put it, want something more "serious." Educational administrators, responding to the needs created by the war, have looked with marked favor upon plans for extension of vocational education. Returning veterans have voiced their intentions of concentrating on an education which will qualify them for new jobs in new industries and better jobs in old ones.

Vocational education conceived as job-training represents the greatest threat to democratic education in our time. It is a threat to democracy because it tends to make the job-trained individual conscious only of his technological responsibilities, but not of his social and moral responsibilities. He becomes a specialist in "means" but indifferent to "ends" which are considered the province of another specialist. The main concern is with "getting a job" and after that with "doing a job" no matter what the political direction and moral implications of the job are. Social programs are judged simply by whether they promise to provide the jobs for which the technician is trained. If a democratic community can supply the opportunity for work, well and good; if it can't, and a totalitarian party or government offers the opportunity, why not? Observers have noted that the technically trained students in institutions of higher education in Germany and Italy have in the mass been much more susceptible to totalitarian propaganda than students whose education has primarily been in the pure sciences. An education that is narrowly vocational, without cultural perspective or social orientation, unillumined by knowledge of large scientific principles considered in a large way, undisciplined by a critical method that sets the range of relevance for methods of technical thinking, is even worse for democratic purposes than a narrow and pure scientific training which, as a special kind of professionalism, is bad in its own way. For the problems on the job are *applications* of scientific knowledge in contexts of social values and human relationships. And it is these which conventional vocational education persistently ignores.

The high incidence of interest in vocational training among youth today reflects the expectation that our economy will have a place for them. The underlying assumption is that the seller's market for the vocationally trained will indefinitely continue in peace as well as in war. This is far from being a sure thing.[2] The history of American capitalism does not provide grounds for great confidence. Vocationally trained talents rusted for almost a decade after the depression. Educators made desperate efforts to revamp curriculums so as to keep youth out of the labor market. We may witness the same thing again. Dearth of vocations may be the most powerful argument against vocational education of the present type. But it would be the weakest argument, and the wisdom it would enforce, besides being costly, would be limited. For, even if prosperity were to continue unabated in years of peace, there is no reason why a truncated vocational education should be substituted for an integrated liberal one. We could well forego the difference in national wealth that would result from keeping young people out of the labor market for a few years, if it added to the immeasurable but more genuine wealth of a well informed, critically minded youth.

Such a critically minded youth would think not only about jobs but about the economy as a whole which provided the jobs and sometimes took them away. Such a youth would not be educated to "adjust" themselves to an economic and social order as if it were as perennial as the course of the stars. They would be encouraged to view it in its historical development. They would be taught to recognize its present-day problems as *occasions for choices* which they, among others, have to make.

[2] For an interesting discussion of the factors bearing on the employability of vocationally trained youth, cf. Selden C. Menefee: *Vocational Training and Employment of Youth*, Research Monograph 25 (Washington, D. C.: U. S. Government Printing Office; 1942).

They would adjust not to the present but to the future as if it were present. To adjust to the future as if it were present is never an automatic reaction. For it is the essence of reflection.

There is a paradox connected with vocational training. The more vocational it is, the narrower it is; the narrower it is, the less likely it is to serve usefully in earning a living. Techniques, know-hows, operative skills change so rapidly in industry that the student who has been trained to perform certain specific tasks runs the risk of suffering from what Veblen called "trained incapacity." This is particularly true for manual crafts. Those who are muscle-bound, either physically or intellectually, must unlearn and relearn, for all their previous vocational training, if they are to continue to earn their living. Proper vocational education stresses doing, of course. Its skills are largely practical, not abstract. But at the same time it must nourish and strengthen powers of flexibility which will enable students intelligently to breast the waves of vocational change. (To a certain extent, this is achieved in the kind of vocational education we call "professional" about which I shall have more to say later.) As we have noted earlier, the impact of automation may so restrict the market for vocations that in the future the entire problem will be transformed into one of creative use of leisure; but until that time comes the issues surrounding vocational education remain acute.

The indictment against vocational education summarized above would be signed with both hands by those who desire to keep liberal education uncontaminated by concern for earning a livelihood. They offer two distinct solutions to the problem. The first is a sharp separation between liberal arts education and vocational education. Liberal arts education above the elementary levels is to be open to anyone who can qualify for it. After it is completed, it may be followed by vocational education. The second solution is much more radical. It has the great merit of making the problem disappear from view. It proposes that vocational education be left to apprentice experience on the job, and that the schools abandon all vocational instruction. I shall discuss this proposal first.

"The thing to do with vocational education," says Robert Hutchins, "is to forget it. As the war training programs in industry have shown, industry can train its hands if it has to, and can do it at lightning speed."[3] If one believes this and also holds, as Dr. Hutchins did a few years ago, that individuals may be divided into those who are "hand-minded" and those who are not, and that the former cannot derive large benefits from a liberal education, the prospects of continued education beyond elementary levels for a large section of the population would appear bleak, indeed. But even if we surrender the view that individuals can be segregated into the "hand-minded" and the verbal-minded, the reason offered for abandoning vocational education is far from convincing.

It is one thing to train men and women in a national emergency for jobs that are temporary and whose temporary character is emphasized in order to draw people away from other pursuits, not needed in war, for which they may have inclination and capacity. The human costs are justified by national need and the economic costs are underwritten by the government. It is quite another thing to make the choice of a lifetime vocation dependent upon the happy chance that individuals who have completed their formal education without any conception of what they are qualified to do will stumble upon just the right thing. After all, the better part of one's waking hours is spent on earning a living unless one is a man of leisure, a prize fighter, or a college president. The very fact that for many people life begins when work is over is a sign that they may have been miscast in their occupation. An

[3] Robert M. Hutchins: "Education for Freedom," *Christian Century,* Vol. 61, No. 46 (November 15, 1944), p. 1314.

intelligent person can hardly give too much thought to the problem of discovering the type of work which will afford him an opportunity to bring his best talents into play and therewith get the sense of significant achievement. Plato's insight is still valid: as a rule most people are happiest doing the work for which they are best qualified. That is why a good education is one which helps the individual discover what he is best qualified to do—no easy task. And that is why a just state strives to help its citizens to realize their voluntary and intelligent choice of vocations by equalizing relevant educational opportunity.

Is it true that training on the job, and at "lightning speed," too, can be adequately substituted for vocational training? It would be hard to distinguish between skilled and unskilled work if this were so. There are two gross confusions in the recommendation that the main varieties of vocational activity should be learned on the job. The first confusion is between certain types of work which almost anyone can adequately do in two weeks of training or less, like punching a machine or doing nurse's aid, and other types of work which require years of preparation, like designing precision tools or medicine. Hazards to health and wealth would mount dangerously if all vocational education took place on the job.

The second confusion is between specific skills, knacks, or tricks of the trade that are always learned best on the job because they change so rapidly, and basic principles whose mastery facilitates the acquisition of these skills. Professional education in medicine, engineering and law is vocational, too. The schools cannot teach the things the physician learns at the bedside, the lawyer in court, the engineer when a particular dam gives way. But without an education in general principles, these practitioners would not know enough to learn from experience. Experience is the source of knowledge, not a guarantee of knowledge; not even total immersion in the stream of experience will fill an empty head.

Those who speak of vocational training on the job would

never apply this piece of wisdom to the professions because professions, forsooth, are not vocations. But they owe us a justification of the distinction. Some vocations demand for their most effective performance more theoretical education than others. But this is only a matter of degree. And, as we shall see, there is some kind of "theoretical" education which should be a *sine qua non* of all "vocational" education.

The more plausible solution presented by academic traditionalists who agree with our indictment of present-day vocational training is to recognize the legitimacy of education for a living but to separate it sharply from liberal education or "education for freedom." The individual is a citizen. He must therefore receive "education for freedom" which is identical for everyone. He is also a worker with a special job to do. He must therefore receive "training for a job" which will not be identical for all individuals. But the two kinds of education have nothing in common. As Alexander Meiklejohn puts it in answering the question how men can be free in modern industrial society:

Now the American theory of freedom answers that question. It does so by distinguishing Education for Freedom from another kind of education. In a free society, we say, every citizen has two different parts to play. He must, therefore, have two different educations. *Unless we can sharply separate these two sets of learning, we cannot understand what the American doctrine of free institutions is.*[4]

To some extent this is a description of the way in which much of vocational education actually functions today. At various levels students are given instruction in certain liberal arts, although the instruction lacks the content and uniformity Mr. Meiklejohn thinks desirable: and there then follows a purely vocational training.

[4] In "Equality and Education," a radio address over MBS, under the auspices of Education for Freedom, Inc., February 14, 1944. My italics.

But it is this very *separation* between the two kinds of education which is pedagogically defective. Vocational education is simply overlaid on liberal education. The bearings of the general ideas and philosophy acquired through liberal education are not integrated with the vocational subject matter at the points where they are most important. Why a man works, the effects of his work, its relation to the tasks of the community are questions quite germane to his vocational activity. They are best studied in specific contexts. The worker remains a citizen while he is at his job. His knowledge of the fact will ofttimes make a difference even to what he does and how he does it. What is called a liberal education should be a continuous process, and there is no reason—except unfamiliarity with the idea—why vocational education should not be liberalized to include the study of social, economic, historical, and ethical questions wherever relevant instead of assuming, as in the existing practice, that education in these matters is something already gone through and forever done with.

Should liberal arts courses be given in addition to the practical courses in vocational education? Or should practical courses be taught in such a way as to introduce historical and social awareness, knowledge of scientific method, and sensitiveness to persons and ethical principles, into consideration of concrete problems? Neither procedure can be laid down as a fixed principle to be followed, although the second is educationally preferable. It depends upon the type of course and the specific subject under study.

The greatest obstacle to this attempt to integrate vocational and liberal education flows from the suspicions of the specialist against introducing anything outside the narrow confines of his specialty. He regards cultural studies in professional schools as a kind of academic boondoggling. It wastes time which in his eyes is already insufficient for the technical matters students should know. The specialist has a natural tendency to view the whole curriculum from the standpoint of his own professional concern. Yet he recognizes how narrowing and educationally disastrous such a perspective is when it is drawn by *other* specialists. This recognition should serve as one of the checks upon his natural appetite. Even in liberal arts colleges, as we have already observed, many subjects, particularly the sciences, are taught from the specialist's point of view to the detriment of broader understanding and abiding interest on the part of students, most of whom, if they become specialists, will be specialists in something else.

Recent tendencies in our best vocational schools, viz., our professional schools, show a growing realization that vocational and liberal education cannot be sharply separated. A dawning perception is now manifest that the best specialist is not necessarily the man who has received the most vocational training. The work of the physician, the work of the lawyer, the work of the engineer in different ways demand a *continuing* familiarity with subjects that would seem to the specialist to be utterly irrelevant to his proper vocational tasks. Yet, as the *Report of the Commission on Medical Education* made clear years ago, "the health" of the individual is as much a social concept as a biological one. It did not say this in so many words, but it is unmistakably implied in the following key passage:

Medical education should emphasize to students the influence of urbanization, industrialization, and present day conditions of living which are important in the causation, treatment, and prevention of disease. These factors must be appreciated if the physician is to perform his function of advising patients in regard to their health problems. The unit of practice, regardless of how medical services are organized or how social organization is changed, will continue to be the individual patient. If the individual is to obtain the most helpful counsel, it is important that the physician be acquainted with the social, economic, and other environmental factors which have an influence on the individual and his health.

These observations, unhappily not yet given force in the curriculum of most medical schools, apply in principle to other fields as well. The best illustrations of legal education today incorporate large bodies of psychological, sociological, and economic analysis into the course of study. The lawyer who knows nothing more than "the law books" is ill-equipped to practice law, handicapped in judging when he is elevated to the bench, and hopelessly at sea when he is called in to advise on, or participate in, the determination of public policy. Although there is wide acceptance of this truth, actual curricular practices lag far behind.[5]

Whether it be business or journalism, government service or social work, engineering or communications, the subject matter of these fields cannot be properly mastered without including much more than vocational techniques. Sometimes the interrelation of studies flows outward, so to speak, from a consideration of problems *within* the technical field, for example in the study of peptic ulcers in medicine or tax laws in accountancy. Sometimes the integration of studies is achieved by considering the relation of the entire field to the social and political context, for example the nature and limits of freedom of expression in radio, cinema, and newspaper. An apparently hackneyed theme like censorship in any one of these fields opens up fundamental philosophical and social questions of the most momentous practical importance. The merely trained, run-of-the-mill technician takes sides on such questions without understanding what it is all about.

Another obstacle to the program of integrating liberal and vocational studies is the almost willful misunderstanding of what the program recommends. Where vocational education is given, aside from the problems that open outward to other

[5] Cf. the ambitious recommendations for the reform of legal education in Harold D. Lasswell and Myres S. McDougal: "Legal Education and Public Policy: Professional Training in the Public Interest," 52 *Yale Law Journal* 203 (1943).

subjects, there are at least two fields in which the integration can take place. The first is the place of the calling within the social economy, and the relation of its professional ethics to the larger issues of social and ethical philosophy. The second is the study of the rationale of scientific method as exemplified in the industrial and technical processes, the inventions and leading ideas, which are used in the work of the special field. This minimum program of interrelation according to John Dewey should constitute an essential part of modern liberal education.

A truly liberal, and liberating, education would refuse to-day to isolate vocational training on any of its levels from a continuous education in the social, moral and scientific contexts within which wisely administered callings and professions must function.[6]

As an illustration of a typical misunderstanding let us consider a direct comment on this position made by Mr. Hutchins:

A truck driver cannot learn to drive a truck by studying physics, chemistry and mathematics. . . . The truck driver, both as truck driver and as citizen, needs to learn to control himself, to take his place in a democratic organization, to discover the meaning and aim of his existence and of the society of which he is a part. Musing over the laws of thermodynamics as he drives is doubtless better than musing over some other things; but it is not likely to prevent him from wrecking both his truck and his life.[7]

Mr. Hutchins' illustration speaks worlds. There is no vocational curriculum on "How to Drive a Truck" in any reputable institution in the country. I doubt whether there is even a course! There are courses in the physics of gas-engines, which is something quite different. But, aside from what we will find

[6] John Dewey: "Challenge to Liberal Thought," *Fortune*, Vol. 30, No. 2 (August 1944), p. 156.
[7] Hutchins: "Education for Freedom," p. 1314.

or not find in our congested curriculums, driving a truck is precisely one of the things which it is *not* the business of vocational education to teach because it is learned in the same way that everybody learns how to drive a car or a bicycle. It is even questionable whether piloting or navigating a plane, which requires skills that cannot be *safely* learned on the job without considerable previous instruction, should by itself constitute the subject matter of a vocational course. Vocational instruction should be give in *the basic principles that govern a whole class of practical skills for which the individual has a bent or interest.* It should not aim at robot-like conditioning of human machines to other machines. Truck driving is as honorable a pursuit as any other but why assume, as Mr. Hutchins apparently does, that whoever begins with it must necessarily remain with it? The function of knowledge of thermodynamics wherever it is pertinent to vocational education is not to be mused over by the driver in the cab of a truck. That would be almost as dangerous as musing over "the meaning and aim of his existence," which Mr. Hutchins apparently would substitute in its stead. The function of such knowledge, when it has been given vocationally, is to enable the truck driver, if he so desires, to master other tasks, to make himself eligible for other vocations, perhaps better paid, perhaps more congenial, perhaps more interesting.

That the truck driver needs to learn to fulfill his duties in a democratic community *both* as truck driver and citizen is a welcome admission by Mr. Hutchins. A continuing education in the problems and issues of democratic social life is precisely what Mr. Dewey recommends as part of the curriculum of all vocational education. The difference between them on this point is that for Mr. Hutchins, since these matters are decidable by eternal truths previously imparted by liberal education on its appropriate level, no further instruction is necessary when job-training occurs; whereas, for Mr. Dewey, questions of social policy and direction, which affect the truck driver as citizen and truck driver, demand a continuous and specifically related study.

This is not confusing liberal and vocational education. It is relating them in such a way that no matter how a man earns his living he will not lose sight of the communal traditions to which he owes his knowledge and skills, the communal responsibilities he shares with his fellows, and the communal tasks to which he can make his distinctive contribution. Vocational education which fails to do this is illiberal and had best be abandoned.

The difficulties of giving organizational form to this integrated curriculum are tremendous. But they must be faced. There are certain healthy developments in existing practice which should be encouraged. In many courses in the liberal arts colleges today an attempt is made to provide either some work experience or firsthand contact with practical activities in which general principles are given application. Instead of being done in a haphazard and episodic way, this should be systematized.[8] During the third and fourth years of the typical liberal arts college, studies are concentrated around a vocational interest but in isolation from the vocation. Guidance by self or others is hardly likely to be sound unless the student is given an opportunity to savor for himself the quality of his prospective vocational career.

The desirable integration between liberal and vocational education cannot be achieved on a wide scale until schools and colleges revolutionize their entire attitude towards the vocational future of their students. They must recognize the vocational future of the students as in large part the present responsibility of the educator. Until now the schools have naturally been most interested in what happens to the student while he is studying. And next to that they have been concerned with the problem of his past education, not to mention

[8] The best example to date of systematization is the Antioch College co-operative work-study program.

the competitive devices of enrolling him. What happens to the student after he has finished his studies or received his diploma is regarded as completely his own individual concern. In one sense, of course, it is. He is on his own. In another sense, he really is not on his own until he is given the chance to bring his capacities into action in the most appropriate place for them. The school co-operating with all agencies of government and industry should help him find that most appropriate place. It is then that the student is truly on his own.

It is not true that the right man always finds the right place by his own unaided efforts. It is just as true that *his* right place is found by someone quicker, someone nearer, someone more adroit in the political handling of people than in the capacities demanded by the job. And for many occupations it is even truer that *his* right place is given to someone else who knows the right people or is born into the right family. And to safe-guard against misunderstanding, let us make perfectly clear that by "the right place" we do not mean a permanent job or slot into which an individual is placed in Platonic fashion in-dependently of his future growth, but a position in which his capacity for further growth is given scope.

It would be utterly utopian to expect every man to find his right place. For many more things determine what constitutes "the right place" than the public good or bad that would result from an individual's filling it. But it is not utopian for educators to accept as a working ideal the general principle of civil service—vocational opportunities should go to those who best merit them. There are many vocational opportunities which are best merited by those who *can get* them, especially when the qualities displayed in the getting are the same as the qualities required in the doing. But there are many more vocational opportunities in which there is no intrinsic connection between the two sets of qualities. It is in respect of these opportunities that the schools must extend their vocational guidance to include voluntary, co-operative placement.

The word to emphasize is *voluntary*. For industries and government agencies will co-operate with schools only if they discover that students recommended as the most likely prospects for vocational openings actually succeed, as a rule, much better than those who are not recommended. The co-operation would be a genuine two-way process with mutual benefits. On a small scale in certain corners of highly technical vocational curriculums this is now being done, primarily for economic reasons. But it is the social and educational validity of the practice which should be stressed, since there are numerous vocations in which the economic advantage, considered only in terms of dollars and cents, cannot be easily assessed. The extension of this practice depends largely upon its recognition by educators and the leaders of the community as an effective method of meeting the rightful claim of the qualified individual for a chance to make good.

It depends upon more than that. As is the case with every other basic educational insight, although it can be given some institutional force here and now, it cannot be built into the fabric of social life without a profound change in the pattern of our economy. It waits for the time when, instead of using individuals as instruments for the production of wealth, the entire economy will be conceived as an instrument for furthering the all-around growth of individuals in a democratic society.

Chapter 10

THE GOOD TEACHER

> "If the modern teacher will think of him-
> self not so much as a schoolmaster but
> as a lifemaster doing from another angle
> what the social worker does in his sphere,
> then he will be striving for all the knowl-
> edge available which could help him in
> his task. He will try to educate a
> generation of youth which combines
> emotional stability with a flexible mind;
> yet he will only succeed if he is capable
> of seeing each of the problems of the
> new generation against the background
> of a changing world."
>
> KARL MANNHEIM

ALL PLANS for educational reforms depend on the teacher for
their proper realization. Unless carried out by a personnel
sincerely imbued with the philosophy animating the reforms
and trained in the arts of effective teaching, they are doomed
to failure. Everyone who remembers his own educational experience remembers teachers, not methods and techniques. The
teacher is the kingpin of the educational situation. He makes
and breaks programs. The initial difficulties and growing pains
of progressive education were primarily caused by a scarcity
of competent teachers. It still remains a source of great difficulty. The recruitment of good teachers has bogged down

partly because hasty *ad hoc* programs have been adopted to meet the urgent needs created by the post-war population explosion. In the main it has been due to the downgrading of the teaching profession itself, both by the detractors of current education and by the impersonal mechanisms of the market which rewards talent in other professions much more handsomely.

The major role of the teacher in the educational process has led some writers to the conclusion that, once students have been assembled for purposes of instruction, the good teacher is all-sufficient. Given a good teacher, they assume, further concern with educational content and method is unnecessary. He has an unfailing natural sense of what it is right to teach and how to teach it. He does not even need a well-appointed classroom. One end of a log will do. Invariably someone will recall an individual of whom he will say: "He did not know anything about pedagogy but he was a great teacher."

Such a position is understandable as a reaction to the view that anybody can be educated to be an educator. It manifests a healthy skepticism toward the overdeveloped curriculums of professional schools of education in which courses are needlessly proliferated. But there is little to be said for it as a serious response to the problems of instruction. If *what* a student learns depends altogether on *who* his teacher is, the result is sure to be a disorderly cross-patch pattern. The traditions and knowledge and skills which our age requires as a common soil in which to cultivate individual variety could hardly be developed. The diversity in temperament of these uniquely endowed persons, and in the direction of their interests as well as ideas, is much greater than among those who cannot spin an entire educational curriculum out of their innards. Such diversity within limits is desirable, provided students are exposed to the varied stimuli of several outstanding personalities. But this is not likely to be the case. For the number of these extraordinary teachers is not large enough to go around. And what the educational system of America needs is at least a million good teachers.

Teaching is an art and like all arts it can be learned with varying degrees of proficiency. Some are so gifted by nature that they can perform as good teachers without learning the arts of teaching, just as some singers can have brilliant musical careers without studying voice culture. On the other hand, there are some individuals who are naturally so handicapped for a teaching career that instruction in the teaching arts can do as little for them as musical study for the tone deaf. Most teachers fall between these two extremes. It is a crime against students to permit individuals of the second kind to enter the ordinary classroom as teachers, no matter how great their gifts may be in other respects or in other fields. Whatever teaching is, it should at least not be an obstruction to learning. But it is certainly no crime, it is not even a hardship, to require of naturally gifted teachers—those who are to the teaching manner born—that they learn the formal rudiments of the art of teaching. They can always improve their skills. An enormous amount of time can be saved by familiarizing oneself with teaching devices and techniques even if one already possesses the educator's insight and an adequate educational philosophy. No one who has not actually attempted to teach the details of a curriculum can properly appreciate the great difference that mastery of specific ways and means can make in motivating interest, facilitating communication, and starting in students a train of thought which runs its course to the click of understanding. There are some things that are best learned *not* on the job. And although we can rely on any teacher to learn by trial and error experience, why should the students pay the price for that experience?

The most satisfactory teaching in American education is being done on the most elementary levels wherever plant facilities are adequate. The least satisfactory teaching is being done on the highest levels. By the "highest" level I mean, not the university, which is or should be primarily an institution for the study and publication of new truth, but the liberal arts college. If we must tolerate a disparity in effective teaching, it is, of course, preferable that the best teaching be done on the lowest level, at the most susceptible age, rather than on the highest, when habits have already hardened. But there is no justification for the disparity, and were the public aware of the actual volume of bad teaching on the college level something would be done to remedy a scandalous situation. Practices are countenanced in colleges which would not be suffered for one moment in any good elementary or secondary high school, and I am not referring here to lecturing and unsupervised study which are sometimes assumed to be the distinctive procedures of college instruction. That some college instruction is excellent does not gainsay the fact that the quality of most of it is bad. Exceptions do *not* prove the rule; neither do they disprove it when the rule is true for the most part.

There are many causes for the comparative deficiencies of college teaching. First is the failure to clarify the function of liberal education, and the dual role the faculty is expected to fill as teachers and research workers. The second is the absence of any training in college teaching, indeed in any kind of teaching, despite the fact that there are certain common psychological and philosophical principles which hold for all varieties of instruction. The third is the indifference, almost hallowed now by tradition, to pedagogical questions. Officially many college teachers, especially if they feel secure because of length of service or publication, profess not to care whether they are good teachers or not. Little serious effort is made to evaluate how well the aims of college instruction are being carried out.

Before discussing the qualities which make for good college teaching and which should serve as criteria in the selection of teachers, I wish to say a brief word about each of the causes of the present state of college teaching.

The historical association between the college and the university has led to administrative confusion about the prerequisites of teaching in both institutions. Insofar as a university is an institution of research, it can use anybody—the blind, the deaf, and the halt—provided only he has a brain. Capacity or incapacity to teach is strictly irrelevant. The only relevant question is whether this man or that can make a contribution to truth. University students are, or should be, mature men and women who are in a sense co-operating with their professors in the quest for truth. They should be expected to discount the personal and superficial mannerisms in those who are guiding their research, and fend for themselves.

The primary function, on the other hand, of the liberal arts teacher is to help young men and women to achieve intellectual and emotional maturity by learning to handle certain ideas and intellectual tools. This requires scholarship, and *familiarity* with current research but not necessarily the capacity to engage productively in it. It is alleged that the good liberal arts teacher will also be interested in doing creative work in his field. This is true for many but cannot be held true for all save by peculiar definition. It is certainly not true—and no one will be bold enough to make it true even by definition—that the good research worker will be an effective undergraduate teacher. Consequently, in selecting college teachers, once scholarly competence in the subject matter has been established, the primary consideration should be whether they give promise of being good teachers—and not, as is the case now, of whether they give promise of being good research workers. There is no necessary connection between a gift for discovery and a gift for lucid explanation, nor even between a gift for discovery and a gift for teaching which evokes the desire for discovery in others. Until the liberal arts college is emancipated from its tutelage to the university, it will not find the teachers it needs.

It is notorious that most college teachers have never taken a course in methods of teaching, even in their own subject matter—and are proud of it. In most institutions, after an instructor survives a preliminary three-year teaching period he can stay put for life. Whether he survives depends basically on his contributions to the world of research—and this world, particularly in the humanities and social sciences, may be served in many curious ways—and only incidentally on his skills as a teacher. Only incidentally—because in few colleges does there exist an established method of evaluating teaching. Hearsay, student popularity, enrollment figures build up a picture, as often false as reliable, of what transpires in the classroom. Teaching is rarely supervised and, when it is, the credentials of the supervisor do not always pass critical muster. In most institutions, visits to the classrooms of one's colleagues are not considered good form. This hypersensitiveness to observation increases when departmental lines are crossed. There are exceptions, of course, but they must not blind us to the general rule.

The indifference and professed contempt of the liberal arts teachers as a group to problems of teaching is partly a reaction to the activities of schools of education. Standards of scholarship are lower in these schools. Not infrequently subject matter courses in the liberal arts are offered in schools of education by individuals who would not qualify on academic grounds for teaching in liberal arts colleges. And yet, when no subject matter courses are offered and instruction is given in *methods* of teaching, these courses are characterized as vapid and empty. In other words, there is a tendency for liberal arts faculties to damn schools of education not only for what they do poorly but for what they do well. There is a legitimate place for schools of education as teacher training institutes, not as rivals to the liberal arts colleges. In addition to stress on methods and techniques, strong curricular emphasis should be placed on the philosophy and psychology of education—themes that are, however, much too important to be left only to schools of education. A more genuine co-operation between liberal arts colleges and schools of education might begin at a point which enables the latter to serve the former by taking over the pedagogic training of its candidates for teacher's posts, leaving certification, on the basis of mastery of subject matter, strictly alone.

The function of the teacher is among the most important in our culture. He not only transmits essential knowledge and skills but, when he takes his calling seriously, strongly influences the formation of habits and the development of a philosophy of life. Yet this high calling is not valued at its true worth by the community nor, ironically enough, by teachers themselves. "Schoolmaster," "professor" are epithets of derision, and the odor of genteel poverty is repellent even to those who regard it as a sign of election. In boom periods the profession is deserted by a scramble for better-paying jobs; in times of depression it is swamped by those who hanker for security. Social disesteem has operated as a principle of selection and bred a type noted for timidity. On paper, college faculties are responsible for all matters pertaining to educational policy and organization; in fact, until recently they have exercised less authority than their glorified clerks. Faculty participation in democratic control of colleges is a favorite theme—for discussion. Here and there in the better-known colleges, faculties have played significant roles in determining educational policy and in providing leadership, but in most situations they are inadequately represented on the governing board.

The first step towards much-needed reforms in the selection of teachers is stabilization of the economic conditions of the profession. This should take place on a plane high enough to liberate teachers from gnawing worry about making ends meet. Once this is achieved, the democratization of the college would be much easier to carry out. For the timidity of teachers grows largely from the knowledge that they face a restricted market for their services in which competitive bidding is only for a few, that administrators fight shy of "troublemakers" even in a good cause, and that the price teachers pay for independence may be loss of a vocation—the only one for which they are trained.

This first step, however, must be accompanied by a rigorous revision of the process by which teachers educate and select their successors. The revision cannot be accomplished overnight, for we must begin where we are and educators themselves must undergo some re-education. What is needed is the *will* to begin, since the knowledge of what constitutes a good teacher is widely distributed. The formulations of the traits which identify the good teacher vary, but it is possible to list those that are observable wherever there is agreement that a good teacher is in action.

A good teacher is not good for all purposes and in all circumstances. In the army, in the church, in the political party, in the penitentiary, as they are presently constituted, a good teacher as we shall define him cannot be used. What makes a good teacher, like what makes a good education, must be considered in relation to certain values. What we are seeking are the criteria of a good teacher in a democratic society whose educational system has embraced the fundamental aims we have previously outlined.

(a) The first criterion is intellectual competence. By this I mean not only the truism that the teacher should have a mastery of the subject matter he is teaching and that he should keep abreast of important developments in his field, but that he should have some capacity for analysis. Without this capacity, he cannot develop it in his students. There are different levels and types of analysis, but what they have in common is an understanding of how to approach problems, of how to take ideas apart, of how to relate our language habits to our intellectual practices. Capacity for analysis is something different from mere possession of the dry-bones and heaps of knowledge. Insofar as the distinction can be made, it is bound up more with method than content. Whatever information a teacher imparts, he must know (and wherever relevant be able to explain) how it is reached, what its validity depends on, and the role of empirical and conventional elements in the answer.

Another element in intellectual competence is a sense of relevant connection. The good teacher should be well oriented in some other fields besides the one in which he may claim to be a specialist. He should be able to follow the thread of an argument or the ramifications of a problem without concern for what a subject is called or for departmental non-trespass signs. I have heard a professor of political science bitterly complain that the economics department was teaching government, too! If the teaching was good, he should have applauded it. On the other hand, not everything in the world is inter-related; and if it were, not all of it would be equally relevant to a specific problem. The most obvious evidence of bad teaching is classroom "thinking by association," in which by a series of grasshopper jumps topics are dwelt on that have no logical connection with each other. The usual result is that the original problem, where there is one, is lost sight of.

Related to intellectual competence is the willingness to countenance, if not to encourage, rational opposition and spirited critical dissent by students. The inquiring mind even among youth sometimes probes deeply. Only a teacher unsure of himself will resent embarrassing questions to which the only honest reply must be a confession of ignorance. Intellectual independence is such a rare virtue that the good teacher positively welcomes it, despite the occasional excesses of youthful dogmatism and exuberance. For many years I refused to believe that any liberal arts teacher would actually penalize a student for intellectual disagreement. But the evidence is overwhelming that in many colleges this is far from exceptional, and that students are often fearful of venturing a defense of ideas and attitudes incompatible with those held by their teachers. In one institution, a teacher of philosophy did not conceal from his students his conviction that to embrace the metaphysics of materialism was to reveal a moral deficiency in character. Anyone who expected a recommendation from him was warned to look to his philosophy. In another institution, a bright member of the Young Communist League bitterly complained to his English teacher who had given him the lowest possible passing grade. In answer, he was told that anyone who believed in dialectical materialism deserved nothing better. A few years later, a young woman who had a perfect record in all her subjects took the same course with the same teacher and received the only C in her college career. On inquiring the reason she was told that no student who *disbelieved* in dialectical materialism deserved anything better. The teacher had become converted and had changed his mind about dialectical materialism—a speculative doctrine really irrelevant to the subject matter of his course. But he had not changed his intellectual ways. He was sincerely convinced that he had the truth on both occasions, but lacked the wit to realize that the students' *reasons* for embracing truth or error were far more important, in their educational experience, than the question of the validity of dialectical materialism. In the last decade, more than one class of students has been punished for the tortuous intellectual pilgrimages of their teachers—particularly at the hands of a certain school of militantly doctrinaire teachers who, despite the fact that their opinions veer as if by order from year to year, regard themselves as qualified to settle the most delicate problems of economics, politics, history, philosophy, and religion with a zeal and confidence that specialists, handicapped by genuine knowledge, shrink from assuming.

Some teachers seem to be constitutionally incapable of tolerating disagreement. Most often their views are deeply conservative. But there are also radical teachers, advanced thinkers about all subjects from sex to salvation, who are just as intolerant of disagreement as the most extreme reactionaries. If anything, their unction and hypocrisy makes their failure a more painful experience. Both types have chosen the wrong profession. In the classroom, the crusader must always play a subordinate role to the teacher and the inquirer. Otherwise he becomes a persecutor in behalf of the old gods or the new.

(b) Intellectual competence is necessary but not sufficient for good teaching. It must be accompanied by a quality of patience towards beginners which accepts as natural the first groping steps towards understanding by the uninitiated. The "simple" and the "obvious" are relative to antecedent skills and knowledge. Failure to see and act on this is responsible for intellectual browbeating by otherwise competent teachers and for the air, deliberately only half-concealed, of suffering the hopeless stupidity of those who are stumbling their way forward. The intellectually quick, and all teachers should be quick, have a tendency towards intellectual impatience. The impatience but not the quickness must be curbed. Patience is something that can be learned, except by certain temperaments who should never be entrusted with a class. Good teaching is not found where a star teacher holds forth for the benefit only of his star pupils, but where some participating response is evoked from every normal member of the class. Nothing is easier than to yield to the pleasures of colloquy with the exceptional students of a class—and nothing is more unfair to the rest, in whom this builds up intense resentment, oddly enough not against the teacher but against their exceptional classmates. Special provision should be made for the instruction of superior students, but a good teacher does not let their special needs dominate the class to the exclusion of the legitimate educational needs of the others.

(c) The third characteristic of good teaching is ability to plan a lesson, without mechanically imposing it on the class, in those subjects where basic materials have to be acquired, and to guide the development of discussion to a cumulative result in subjects in which the seminar method is used. The bane of much college teaching is improvisation. Improvisation is not only legitimate but unavoidable in motivating interest and finding points of departure or illustration for principles. But it cannot replace the planful survey of subject matter and problems, nor provide direction to discussion. It is delightful to follow the argument wherever it leads. But it must be an argument. And it should lead somewhere.

Where improvisation is chronic and draws its materials from autobiography, teaching sinks to its lowest level. In my own experience I recall teachers who rarely knew what they were going to talk about before they came to class. Usually they would talk about themselves or their families. Over the years, when members of their successive classes came together, they were able to construct a fairly accurate composite family portrait. The personalities of such teachers rarely possessed a richness or power that might justify taking themselves as subject matter. The contempt in which intelligent students held them was checked only by the teachers' power to distribute grades— a power which they wielded with a whimsical irresponsibility.

Naturally, the responsibility of the teacher for the progressive organization of subject matter varies with elementary and advanced classes, and he will proceed differently in presenting a lecture and in conducting a tutorial. Nothing I have said suggests the necessity of a detailed lesson plan which is as often a drawback as an aid even in the secondary schools. What the teacher must aim at is to make each class hour an integrated experience with an aesthetic, if possible a dramatic, unity of its own. Without a spontaneity that can point up the give and take of discussion, and a skill in weaving together what the students themselves contribute, preparation will not save the hour from dullness. The pall of dullness which hangs over the memories of school days in the minds of many unfortunately envelops the whole question of education.

(d) Another important quality the good teacher possesses is knowledge of human beings. He is in a sense a practical psychologist. He knows something more about people than the laws of their learning curves, and what he knows he has not found in textbooks on psychology. The more one studies students, the more differences they reveal. These differences need not be relevant to what they are trying to learn; but sometimes they are. A teacher devoid of this knowledge cannot solve the problem of motivation or evoke full participation from his class. Nor can he tell when to temper the wind, when to let it blow, when to build up self-assurance in the pathologically shy, when to deflate the bumptious. Unable to diversify his challenges, he cannot teach with proper justice and discipline in a class of miscellaneous talents. He may have a standard for the group; he should have a standard for each individual in terms of his special needs—whether they be disabilities or advantages.

Except on the frontiers of knowledge, subject matter cannot be continuously fresh. The great bulk of what is taught to students in every institution except the graduate schools of universities is "old stuff" to their teachers. To stay intellectually alive as one traverses familiar ground year in and year out is not easy. It can be done, of course, by rotating assignments, by taking sabbaticals and, most important of all, by strong theoretical interests in one's own field and related fields. But to stay intellectually alive in the classroom is something else again. Yet for the sake of students one must be alive there if nowhere else. The new developments in one's field seldom bear upon the fundamentals of college instruction, and the minutiae of scholarship have meaning only to those who are already well instructed.

The secret of intellectual vitality in the classroom, when a theorem is being derived for the twentieth time or when an elementary point in the grammar of a foreign language is being explained or when the nerve of an old philosophic argument is being laid bare, lies in experiencing the situation as a fresh problem in communication rather than one in personal discovery. Or, putting it a little differently, it consists in getting the students to reach the familiar conclusion with a sense of having made their own discovery. The task is to make as many as possible see as much as possible of what they have not seen before. It is this perennial challenge, which cannot be adequately met without a knowledge of people, that keeps the good teacher alive. If he does not recognize it, he is a pedagogical automaton, and almost always a bore.

Where knowledge has not yet been won and the authority of method does not point to inescapable and well-tested conclusions, the love of truth can be relied on to generate its own enthusiasm. But where knowledge is already warranted by methods that are themselves warranted, and where originality is likely to be little more than a craving for attention or an expression of conceit, the love of truth by itself cannot be relied upon to make a lesson exciting. There is something suspicious about any mind that can be thrown into raptures of enthusiasm at stated intervals, and in pretty much the same language too, by the statement of truths he has been purveying to students term in, term out. Such enthusiasm is synthetic and the students know it.[1]

There is a crackle of interest always present in the classroom of a good teacher no matter how trite or timeworn the theme. It is supplied not merely by the teacher's love of truth but by the students' desire to discover the truth, and by the teacher's

[1] There is a story told on the campus of an eastern college of an art teacher, now happily no longer teaching, who used to lecture by what might be called the method of sustained respiration. In treating of a certain figure in the history of art, at a fixed point in his course, he would draw a deep breath and, in a mounting crescendo, declaim the artist's wonders. One day he began as usual. "He had no sense of form, he had no sense of color, he had no sense for religion or morals, he broke all the rules of good drawing . . ." and before he could finish, back chorused the class with his punch-line, "But my God! could that man paint!"

interest in that desire and in the arts of gratifying it. In the end, the good teacher makes himself superfluous and the good student learns the art of self-education. But it is literally in the end.

(e) He knows man best who loves him best. A teacher cannot love all his students, nor is it wise to love any of them. The knowledge appropriate for good teaching requires an emotion not so strong as love but also not so irrational. This emotion is sympathy. The good teacher must like people and be interested in them as people, and yet he need not like or be interested in everyone. I am speaking of a general personality trait. It need not find universal expression in every action. But without it an intellectually competent teacher may do more harm than good. There is such a thing as sadism in educational life. Teachers have enormous powers to make students miserable; and, where they are chosen haphazardly, there will always be some who will visit their frustrations and disappointments upon those before them, usually under the guise of being strict disciplinarians. The incidence of insanity is higher among teachers than in any other profession, and the academic community is no freer from phobias like anti-Semitism than the rest of the community. It requires only one teacher to ruin a student's career.

Sympathy is a positive attitude of imaginative concern with the personal needs of others. Benevolent neutrality and mechanical application of rules, no matter how scrupulous, are no substitutes for it. If justice is based on understanding, then without sympathy there cannot be true justice. For understanding is never complete without the sympathy that awakens our organs of perception. Those who teach large numbers and never get to know their students have a tendency to regard all but a brilliant few as a dull, cloddish mass. Reduce the number in each class, shorten the perspective, and no one worthy of being a teacher will fail to see the interesting variety of potentiality in every group. Even outside the classroom it takes two people to make one bore. And, next to ideas, persons are the most interesting things in the world. In each person there is some unique quality of charm, intelligence, or character, some promise and mystery that invites attention and nurture. The teacher who seeks it will find it.

Students respond to sympathy for their special intellectual needs like plants to sunshine and rain. They undertake more and achieve more. A certain danger exists that they may at the beginning undertake tasks in order to please their teacher or not to disappoint him but, if proper guidance is furnished, their own sense of growing mastery of a task and of its increasing significance provides intellectual momentum. The function of the teacher at this point is unobtrusively to raise the stick of achievement higher and to offer criticism without killing self-confidence. Students rarely disappoint teachers who assure them in advance that they are doomed to failure. They do not, of course, always live up to the more optimistic expectations of their teachers but they invariably do the better for it.

It is easy to caricature what I am saying by pretending that this is a demand that the teacher be a nurse or a psychiatrist to his students or that he serve literally *in loco parentis*. It would be helpful, naturally, if a teacher were to know the chief relevant facts about those students who need psychiatrists or nurses, if only to put them in proper professional hands and thus prevent them from serving as a drag on other students. But the teacher should not essay the role of amateur psychiatrist or nurse. His sympathy must be primarily directed to his students as growing intellectual organisms in a growing intellectual community, in the faith that they will become integrated persons capable of responsible choice. He cannot cope with all their emotional needs or assume the responsibilities of family and society, priest or judge. He must be friendly without becoming a friend, although he may pave the way for later friendship, for friendship is a mark of preference and expresses itself in indulgence, favors, and distinctions that unconsciously find an invidious form. There is a certain distance between teacher and student, compatible with sympathy, which should not be broken down—for the sake of the student. A teacher who becomes "just one of the boys," who courts popularity, who builds up personal loyalties in exchange for indulgent treatment, has missed his vocation. He should leave the classroom for professional politics.

What I have said flows from the faith that imaginative sympathy towards the needs of the individual student, based on an intelligent appraisal of his equipment and achievements, will enhance his powers of growth. This faith may appear utopian or romantic. Those who are so impressed usually confuse two things: whom we shall teach and how we shall teach. If, at any level or for a specific purpose, a student is uneducable, a large assumption but sometimes obviously true, he should either be directed to a field in which he is educable or committed to an institution for the feeble-minded, for that is where people who are absolutely uneducable belong. But so long as a teacher finds himself before a class in which there are varied talents, varied capacities for educability, he is under an obligation to help each one develop the best within him. That is what he is there for. If he accepts his obligation gladly and not as a chore, he will find that the results are worth the effort.

What to teach and how to teach must be distinguished from the problem of certification of student competence. Competence is a relation not only to subject matter but to comparative performance and to a set of conditions, far from fixed, defined by the nature of the task for which competence is required. There is also something that may be called a "conventional" element in the determination of competence. This is clearest when, because only a certain number can be certified, all whose achievements fall below this number are failed even though their achievements surpass those of individuals who have been previously certified. Competence established by position on a comparative scale can be ascertained even by those who are not teachers. What the teacher alone can supply is testimony of intellectual and personal qualities which he is uniquely qualified to observe. This testimony together with other data of measurable competence should determine the educational decision to advance, to hold, or to transfer the individual student. The basic consideration should be: what action will educationally most profit the individual without too great a cost to others? Detailed rules cannot wisely be drawn *in abstracto*. For all sorts of factors, sometimes even the state of the nation, may affect their formulation.

To develop the best in each student, therefore, emphatically does not mean that the teacher believes that all students are equally good, or that when he must rate them he should rate them all in the same way, or that he must sacrifice "standards" —a blessed word which is the hardest-worked substitute for thinking on educational matters among college teachers. Those who mouth the word most loudly as soon as any proposal is made to liberalize liberal education do not know what "standards" actually are, their source, their history, and that "standards," too, must face a test which requires other standards. They usually maintain that their own standards are absolute and objective, but no two of them agree with each other. It is notorious that one college's *Pass* student is another's *cum laude*, and that even in the same college one professor's *A* is another's *C*. Time and again it has been experimentally proved that the same teacher, irrespective of subject matter, rates the same paper differently, when he has not identified it as such, depending on matters that have nothing to do with education. Those who talk in absolutes here are only absolutizing their own subjectivity. Those who are militantly self-righteous about the number of students they regularly fail rarely stop to ask whether the fault lies in their own teaching or in the kind of standards they are using. I have heard teachers urge the imposition of standards which would obviously have barred *them* from any possibility of a college education if the proposed standards had been applied in all fields when they were students.

The teacher's working standards in the classroom should be distinct from the rules that determine the next step in the educational career of the student, i.e., whether he is to pass or fail. These working standards cannot be adjudged "high" or "low," for they should be nothing else but the realization of the fundamental ends of the educational process itself through the use of the most appropriate means that will insure the maximum intellectual growth of every student entrusted to him. If these are his working standards, the teacher will never be satisfied that this maximum has been finally reached. For with every intellectual achievement new vistas of knowledge open before us.

(f) The good teacher, to close our inventory of his traits, possesses vision. It is the source of both his intellectual enthusiasm and his detachment in the face of inevitable failures and disappointments. Without vision he may become a kindly technician, useful in a limited way. But he cannot inspire a passion for excellence. The vision may take many forms. It may be a doctrine—but he must not preach it. It may be a dream—but he must not keep talking about it. It may be a hope, an ambition, a work in progress, so long as it is not merely personal and has a scope or sweep of some imaginative appeal. But it must not obtrude itself into the details of instruction. Its presence should be inferrable from the spirit with which the instruction is carried on. It should operate in such a way as to lift up the students' hearts and minds beyond matters of immediate concern and enable them to see the importance of a point of view. Wherever an intellectually stimulating teacher is found, there will also be found some large perspective of interest that lights up the corners of his subject matter. If students catch fire from it, it should not be in order to believe some dogma but to strengthen them in the search

for truth and to become more sensitive to visions that express
other centers of experience.

The best teacher possesses all of the qualities we have mentioned to a pre-eminent degree. But the best teacher is to be
found only in a Platonic heaven. Good teachers, however, who
exhibit some or all of these qualities are to be found on earth.
They can become, can be helped to become, and can help
others to become, better teachers. If a resolute beginning is
made by those who educate and select teachers, in time the
community will discover that a new spirit and morale is abroad
in the teaching profession. It will discover that a good teacher
is a *dedicated* person, strong in his faith in what he is doing,
worthy not only of honor in a democracy but of a place in
its councils.

When educational laymen speak of the non-material rewards
of good teaching, only too often their kindly observations are
fumbling words of consolation for the presumed deprivation
of careers isolated from the dramatic struggles of "real" life.
There *are* deprivations entailed by the profession of teaching
but these are not among them. Most teachers are not men of
action by temperament and self-selection keeps them out of
the forays and battles of daily life. And no matter what their
temperament, a lifetime of exposure to immature minds unfits
them for positions in politics or business in which risks must
be run and quick decisions taken before all the evidence is in.
Teachers unaware of the limiting effect of the very fact of
pedagogic excellence upon their habits of mind tend to take
themselves too seriously and to regard the world as a classroom
waiting for the proper lessons to solve the problems of adult
experience. A sense of humor about themselves is the best assurance of a sense of proportion in these matters—a safeguard
against taking themselves too seriously as well as against vain
regrets. When a man becomes a teacher it is extremely unlikely

that the world has lost a great political leader or prophet.

Every choice among viable alternatives involves a sacrifice of some genuine good. Teachers, like others, make sacrifices in the selection and pursuit of their calling. To the individual who has found himself in teaching these sacrifices are far from galling. For if he has found himself in his calling, in all likelihood he has had a successful career. It is not the emoluments and social status or holiday words of community praise which are criteria of success for him. Rather is it a twofold satisfaction. First, he is aware of being a part of a continuing tradition which, no matter how humble his role in it, connects the great minds of the past with those of the present and future. Second, although the teacher like the actor is a sculptor in snow and can leave no permanent monument of his genius behind, he can reach the minds of those who will survive him, and through them affect the future. The lives of most people would have been pretty much the same no matter who their teachers were. But there are a sufficient number of men and women in the world who can truthfully testify to the determining and redetermining role which some teachers played in their lives. To very few is it given to exercise this influence. The opportunity to do so is a measure both of the power of the teacher and of his responsibility.

INDEX

A NOTE ON THE TYPE

THE TEXT of this book was set on the Linotype in
JANSON, a recutting made direct from type cast
from matrices long thought to have been made by
the Dutchman Anton Janson, who was a practicing type founder in Leipzig during the years
1668–87. However, it has been conclusively dem-
onstrated that these types are actually the work
of Nicholas Kis (1650–1702), a Hungarian, who
most probably learned his trade from the master
Dutch type founder Dirk Voskens. The type is
an excellent example of the influential and sturdy
Dutch types that prevailed in England up to the
time William Caslon developed his own incom-
parable designs from these Dutch faces.

Composed, printed, and bound by
The Haddon Craftsmen, Inc., Scranton, Pa.
Typography and binding design by
HERBERT H. JOHNSON